Quick Games
from Trash

By
Chris Sowada

Cover Illustration by
Darcy Bell-Meyers

Inside Illustrations by
Ann Lutnicki

Publisher
Instructional Fair • TS Denison
Grand Rapids, Michigan 49544

Permission to Reproduce

Dedication

To my husband, Patrick, for all your love and support

Acknowledgments

This book would not have been possible without the support of my husband, Patrick, and my three children, Jennifer, Christopher, and Zachary, who willingly put up with my collection of "trash." I would also like to thank three very special friends, Marsha, Shirley, and Susan, for their laughter, understanding, and encouragement. Over the years I also have been inspired by many teachers and students with whom I have come in contact. Each idea in this book has been an activity I have used with my students.

C. S.

Credits

Author: Chris Sowada
Cover Illustrations: Darcy Bell-Myers
Inside Illustrations: Ann Lutnicki
Project Director & Editor:
    Debra Olson Pressnall
Cover Art Production: Darcy Bell-Myers
Graphic Layout: Deborah Hanson McNiff

About the Author

Chris Sowada has worked for more than 20 years in the field of education. During part of that time she taught first and second grade students in Iowa and Wisconsin before relocating to Clarksville, Tennessee. After taking a break to spend time raising her three children, she became involved in early childhood education by teaching preschool. She is now director of a preschool program and also teaches a kindergarten class. Not only is active in providing resources for her classroom that cost very little, she also enjoys working with other teachers by presenting workshops for early childhood educators in the Nashville area.

Table of Contents

Introduction

As educators, we are challenged to teach children at younger ages. Many children are in school settings early as their mothers join the workforce. As a result, children in early childhood programs are exposed to much information and have many rich learning opportunities. How can we keep their interest and motivate them?

As educators we are also challenged by the cost of learning games, manipulatives, and art materials. As a director of a preschool, I realize there is a vast quantity of wonderful products that are available to me but I am strictly limited with a small budget. How do we provide items to motivate students and keep the expenses down?

The answer to both questions is to make your own learning games and activities with items that many people throw into the trash. RECYCLE those items. The cost is minimal and the wealth of creative activities for your class can keep your students challenged and interested—and it is FUN!

I hope the ideas that are offered in this book will motivate you to create many new games and activities for your classroom. These games can also teach your students a valuable lesson—to recycle. There is a wealth of trash in our world, so have fun and turn some of it into learning opportunities!

Before you begin making games from discarded materials or inexpensive items, you must realize ANYTHING can be made into a learning activity. Once you open yourself to that realization, your creativity will flourish.

There are other considerations to keep in mind. You must be willing to collect items to be used later—either for an activity you plan to do or because you are not quite sure what to do with the items right now. You will need to plan for the storage of your completed activities. Some classrooms have storage areas, but for most teachers their homes also become storage areas. So plan an area that can be designated for the storage of your "treasures." You must allow some time to SHOP! Take a minute to look over clearance sections, discarded items, or stop at neighborhood garage sales. During those few minutes you may discover a wealth of inexpensive materials. It also is helpful to find a partner with whom you can share ideas and materials. You may not know quite what to do with an item but your partner might have an idea. Each time I meet with my "partner" I become motivated to do more!

The materials used in this book are items that can be easily collected with the help of parents or colleagues. The process is easy to start. Send a letter to parents/guardians listing the items you need and then place a collection box in your classroom. Children love to help and soon you will have a great collection of items for new activities!

Tips on Construction and Organization

All teachers are busy! It takes time to make your classroom an exciting learning environment. One way to handle this task easily is by GETTING ORGANIZED! It may take some time to set up your system, but the time saved later is well worth the effort. Follow the tips below when organizing your classroom and materials.

Organization

1. Decide first how your classroom is already setup. Do you play activities around themes, letter of the week, or by different skills? Set up your games and activities based on your existing system. Store your games in containers or boxes according to your system. Each activity is ready to use as you need it.

2. Set up a file system. Get a file box and create a folder for each topic. When you have a new idea, place it in the appropriate file folder. Make notes on construction and what materials you will need. When you are ready to prepare your classroom for that particular skill or theme, pull out your file and you will have new ideas at your fingertips. Plan to look at your file a week or two ahead so you will have time to prepare any new games or activities.

3. As you see items that lend themselves to a game or activity you might want to make, place them in a box and then write a note in your file system. A clearance table at a store can provide many new items at a time before you are ready to prepare the game. By having a collection box and your idea noted in the file system, you will have the materials handy when you do have the time to work on the game.

4. Create a collection box for items that parents can gather for you. Let parents know at the beginning of the school year what items you need. As you collect enough items, inform the parents so you will not have too many things to store.

5. Use the collection of items from parents as a natural lesson on counting and sorting for your students. Assign children to be responsible for counting, sorting, and putting away items brought in. Children love to help and it can be a learning experience as well as a great help for the teacher.

Storage

1. Decide which areas you have in your classroom and home that you can dedicate to storage. If you have shelf space, use boxes that can stack. Label EACH box so that the contents are clearly visible. You do not want to spend valuable time hunting for your games or activities. Organize them as you did your file system.

2. Small items can be stored in cans, such as potato chip cans. Glue an item to the lid so you can quickly identify what is inside the can. Children then can also locate the items quickly for games or can help put them away as the items are collected.

3. If you have available closet space or if you can hang a dowel from the ceiling, you can create a storage area with bags or pillowcases. Fold the corners of a pillowcase over a hanger and pin them. Now your homemade storage area is ready for games and activities.

Additional Quick Tips

1. Try to laminate your games and activities before adding the content material. Print the skill with permanent marker. Later the wording can be easily removed with fingernail polish remover. This allows you to vary your games according to your students' abilities. It also makes your games more versatile by being able to use them in different subject areas.

2. When making games out of lids, such as shoe boxes, try to find several lids that match one box bottom. This way you only need to store one box bottom with several lids.

3. ALWAYS check your games before putting them away. Count the game pieces to make sure everything is there. The start of the game is not a good time to discover a missing piece!

4. Always make extra pieces for a game to allow for those pieces that turn up missing! SAVE your patterns! You may create a game one year, try to use it at another time, and realize you need more game boards or game pieces. With the patterns at your fingertips, you will save yourself a great deal of time.

CAN YOU FIND IT?

Language Arts

Skill:
Alphabet recognition

Materials Needed:
- clear adhesive plastic or laminating material
- construction paper
- facial tissue
- glue or masking tape
- one grease pencil for each child working on the activity
- permanent marker
- several cereal boxes (popular children's cereal, if available)
- small colored dot stickers (different color for each cereal box panel)
- pattern page 9

Directions for Assembly:
1. Collect several different kinds of cereal boxes and cut off the front panel of each to make the game boards.
2. Place a colored dot sticker in the top corner of the panel. Make sure each one has a different colored sticker.
3. Cover each panel with clear adhesive plastic or laminating material.
4. To prepare the task cards, make one copy of the pattern (see page 9) for each panel.
5. Select letters that can be found on the cereal box panel and then print them on the task card.
6. Finish by placing an identical sticker on the top corner of the task card that corresponds with the cereal box panel.
7. Repeat the procedure for the other cereal box panels.
8. Mount the task cards on construction paper and then laminate or cover them with clear adhesive plastic for durability.
9. Using construction paper and glue or masking tape, create a pocket on the back of each game board to store the task cards.

How to Play:

1. Depending on the number of game boards, invite a small group of children to each select a game board. It works best to have an extra game board for the children to use when finished with their work.
2. Have each child remove the task card from the pocket.
3. Using the grease pencil, find and circle the letters on the cereal box panel that match the letters on the task card.
4. When the child has completed the task card, have him use the facial tissue to remove the grease pencil marks and then select a different game board to continue working.

Other Ideas for Cereal Boxes!

For children who are not yet ready to find alphabet letters, have them find pictures or shapes on cereal boxes. To do this, collect two of each type of cereal box. Cut the shapes or pictures from one box, leaving the matching box intact. Glue the pictures or shapes to a task card. Laminate or cover all of the game components with clear adhesive plastic.

Perhaps the children may be interested in finding words. Using your collection of cereal box panels, select words for the children to find. Print the chosen words on the task cards and laminate all game pieces. Breakfast will never be the same for the children in your classroom!

Can You Find It?

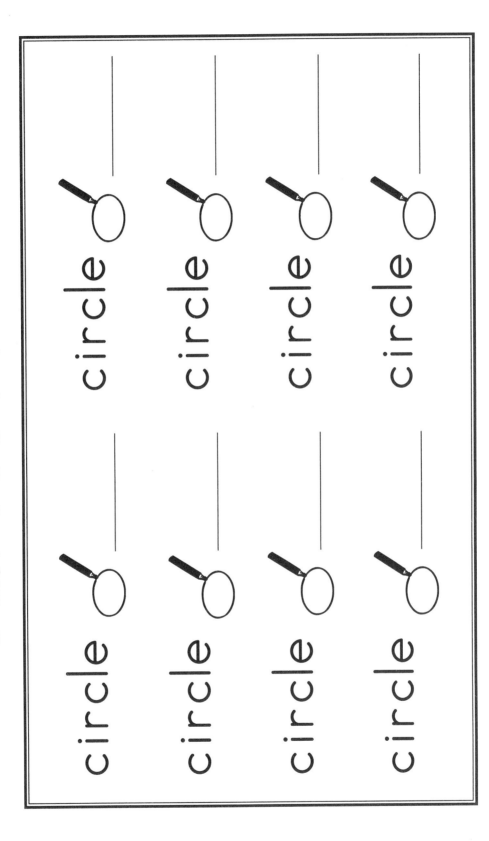

circle _____   circle _____

circle _____   circle _____

circle _____   circle _____

circle _____   circle _____

IF18974 *Quick Games from Trash*

ALPHABET IN A CAN

Language Arts

Skill:
Alphabet recognition

Materials Needed:
- 26 large white beans or snap-on lids (milk or water jug caps)
- construction paper
- glue or tape
- large safety pin or paper clip
- one empty potato chip can with plastic lid
- paper fastener
- permanent marker
- watercolor markers

Directions for Assembly:

1. Cut the construction paper to fit around your can. Using the watercolor markers decorate the paper with alphabet letters along with an interesting design.

2. Laminate the paper or cover it with clear adhesive plastic and then attach it around the can.

3. Using the permanent marker, write the alphabet letters on each bean or snap-on lid for game pieces. *Note:* This game can be played with several variations, using only uppercase letters or lowercase letters or by providing the entire set of both cases. If the children are only working with a portion of the alphabet, then provide just those letters.

4. To finish the game components, change the lid from the can into a spinner. Using a permanent marker, divide the lid into three sections. Print the number 1 in one section, the number 2 in another, and the number 3 in the last section.

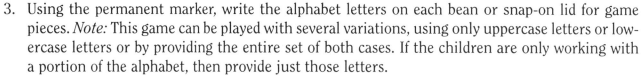

5. Using the brad, secure the large safety pin or paper clip to the middle of the lid for the spinner.

6. Finish by placing the game pieces inside the container and securing the lid on top.

How to Play:

1. Select three or four children to play the game.
2. Remove the lid from the container. Have a child flick the spinner and read the number indicated.
3. Each player takes a turn and draws the corresponding number of game pieces from the container.
4. The child must identify the alphabet letter on each game piece. Each letter that is correctly identified is kept by the player. If she cannot correctly identify the letter name, the game piece is returned to the container.
5. Play continues for a predetermined time or until the last letter has been drawn.
6. The child that named the greatest number of alphabet letters is the winner.

Other Ideas!

What else can be in the can? Sight words, math facts, shapes—the possibilities are endless! The game can be made and played in the same way with only the cover of the can and the game pieces changing to reflect the skill you want to reinforce.

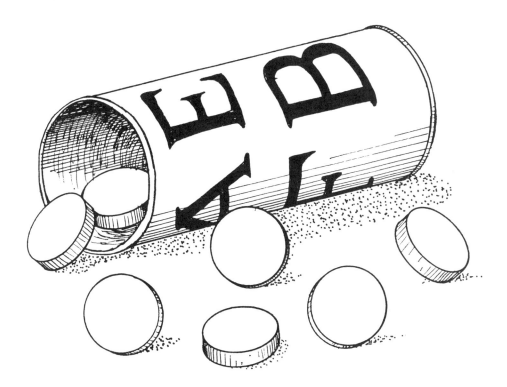

LEAPIN' FROGS

Language Arts

Skills:
Alphabet recognition
Capital and lowercase letter match

Materials Needed:
- beanbags or small plastic frogs that "leap" when pressed
- old window shade, shower curtain, or vinyl tablecloth for game mat
- one wrapping paper cardboard tube and rubber band
- pattern page 14
- permanent markers

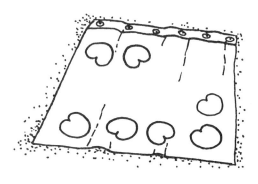

Directions for Assembly:
1. Using permanent markers, draw 26 lily pads on the game mat (shower curtain, window shade, or table-cloth). See pattern page 14 for the suggested shape. Add additional details such as small dragonflies, fish leaping from the water, small frogs, and flowers for a few lilypads to create a charming scene.
2. Write an alphabet letter on each lily pad using the permanent marker. *Note:* You may write both capital and lowercase letters on the lily pads, or you may wish to reinforce only one or the other. See illustrations:

Example 1	Example 2	Example 3

3. To store your game board, wrap it around the cardboard tube and secure it with a rubber band.

How to Play:

1. Select a small group of children to play the game.
2. Each child takes a turn by helping the frog "leap" to a lily pad and naming the alphabet letter shown on the pad. This is done by tossing the beanbag or pressing a purchased plastic frog to make it "leap."
3. Play continues for a predetermined of time or until each alphabet letter has been named.
4. Follow-up with individual folder games on page 15.
5. *Variation:* This can become a teacher-directed activity by asking the child to find a specified letter and then "leap" the frog to it. Example: "Can you make your frog leap to the letter C?"

Other Ideas!

Of course, sight words, math facts, and number recognition (small or large numbers) can also be reinforced with this leap frog game.

FROGS IN THE POND

Skills:

Alphabet recognition
Capital and lowercase letter match
Alphabetical order

Materials Needed:

- 26 snap-on lids (milk or water jugs)
- colorful file folder
- die (numbered 0–5) and two game markers
- glue
- patterns pages 14, 16-17
- resealable plastic bag
- scissors
- two sheets of green construction paper
- watercolor markers

Directions for Assembly:

1. Photocopy the game board patterns on pages 16-17. Color the copies with markers and then mount them on the file folder to make a game board.
2. Make 26 frogs (pattern page 14) on green paper, cut them out and then mount them on the snap-on lids.
3. Determine which skill the children will practice with this game—matching uppercase and lowercase letters in random order or alphabetical order. Print a capital letter on each lily pad and the corresponding lowercase letter on a frog.
4. Store the frogs in a resealable plastic bag.

How to Play:

1. Independent activity: The child removes the frogs from the bag and matches each frog to the corresponding lily pad.
2. A partner game: Both children select objects for game markers and place them near the first lily pad (upper lefthand corner). Have the children take turns rolling the die and moving the game markers the corresponding number of lily pads. When a player lands on a lily pad, the player must find the matching corresponding letter on a frog and set it aside. If the letter on the frog is incorrect, the player must return her game marker to the lily pad from where she started during this turn.
3. When both players have moved through the pond, invite them to count how many frogs they collected.

Start

Stop

MILK CAP SEQUENCE

Language Arts

Skill:

Letters in alphabetical order

Materials Needed:

- 24 screw-on or snap-on lids (milk or water jugs), eight caps each in three different colors
- clear adhesive plastic or laminating material
- glue
- pattern pages 20–25
- permanent markers
- scissors
- three colorful file folders
- three resealable plastic bags

Directions for Assembling:

1. Copy the patterns on pages 20–25 and cut out.
2. Mount the matching game boards on file folders. If you are able to use three colors of plastic caps for your game pieces, then adhere a matching colored dot to the corresponding file folder game to let the child know which pieces correspond with each game.
3. Cover the game boards with clear adhesive plastic or laminating material.
4. For Game A, use a permanent marker to write the following letters on lids of one color:

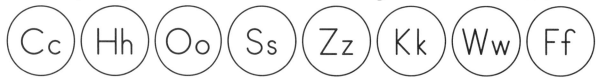

5. For Game B, use a permanent marker to write the following letters on lids of one color:

6. For Game C, use a permanent marker to write the following letters on lids of one color:

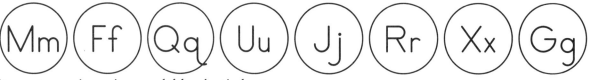

7. Store game pieces in resealable plastic bags.

How to Play:

1. Let each child select a file folder and plastic bag with matching game pieces.
2. To play, the children place the game pieces on the corresponding circles to arrange the letters in alphabetical order.

Other Ideas!

If you are unable to obtain plastic jug caps of different colors, you may attach a sticker, write a number or draw a shape on the inside of the milk cap to help the child find the matching pieces to each game board. Place the corresponding sticker, shape, or number onto the corresponding game board before laminating it.

If you do not want to use plastic lids, cut out circles from poster board, then write the letters on them before laminating them. *Note:* Plastic jug caps are easier to pick up and place on the game board and are not as easily lost, but paper circles will work.

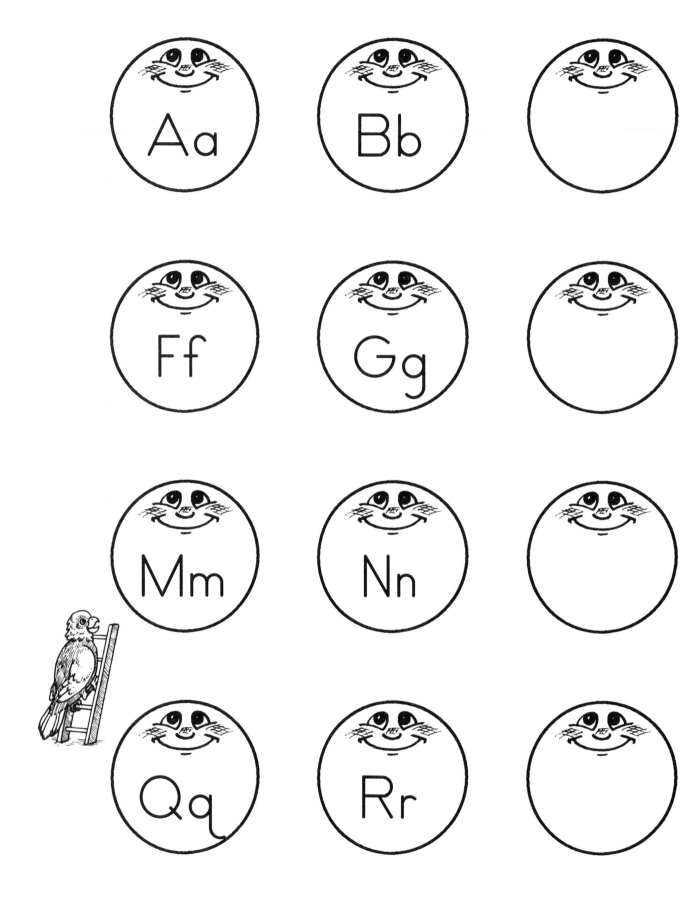

ABC VEGETABLES

Language
Arts

Skill:
Alphabetical order of words

Materials Needed:
- clear adhesive plastic
- eight or more paper labels from vegetable cans (14.5 oz. size), one of each variety
- glue
- oaktag or construction paper
- pattern pages 28–30
- permanent markers
- resealable plastic bag or small box
- scissors
- three-minute timer

Directions for Assembling:
1. Remove the labels from four different vegetable cans. Trim each label into a rectangle approximately 4" (102 mm) in height and 3" (76 mm) in width so that the front of the label clearly shows the name of the vegetable as well as fitting on the can pattern (see page 28).
2. Using a permanent marker, outline the first letter of the vegetable name you wish the children to use when alphabetizing. Some examples: If the vegetable label shows "Peas," highlight the "P." If the label says "Cut Green Beans," highlight the "G" in "Green."
3. Duplicate copies of the can pattern on construction paper for the vegetable labels you have collected. Cut out the can patterns.
4. Glue the vegetable labels onto the can patterns to make playing cards.
5. If you choose to make this activity self-checking, turn the picture cards face down and number them in alphabetical order. Write number 1 on the first vegetable card, write number 2 on the second and so on. The children can turn the activity cards face down to check their work. If the numbers are in numerical order, the words were alphabetized correctly.
6. Cover the playing cards with clear adhesive plastic for durability.
7. Create additional sets by choosing different combinations of labels. For example: Set A may contain labels for corn, peas, beans, carrots. Set B may contain labels for okra, yams, tomatoes, and corn. Set C may contain labels for peas, yams, beans, and tomatoes. Mount each set on different colored construction paper.
8. Place the sets of cards in a plastic bag or a small box for storage.
9. Photocopy the game board pattern pages and mount them on a file folder.

How to Play:

1. Invite two children to work with the cards or provide the materials in a center where one child can work independently.
2. Have each child select a set of cards and then start the timer. Encourage children to place the pictures in alphabetical order on the game board within a specified time.
3. When finished, they can turn over the cards to check their work.

Other Ideas!

Instead of alphabetizing words, have the children arrange letters in alphabetical order. To prepare the materials, collect 26 vegetable labels of various kinds. Follow the directions for making the game cards on the preceding page. Change the labels by printing large-sized letters (A–Z) on them instead of high-lighting letters. Now young learners can show the alphabet from A to Z. To make the cards self-checking, number the backs of the cards (1–26) to show the correct sequence.

LID WHEELS

Language Arts

Skill:
Capital and lowercase letter match

Materials Needed:
- craft knife
- paper fastener
- permanent markers
- scissors
- two clear plastic lids in different sizes (ice cream bucket, margarine tub), one set per player

Directions for Assembly:
1. Trim off the lip of each lid, leaving two plastic circles.
2. Cut a hole in the center of each lid with a craft knife.
3. Using the paper fastener, attach the small circle on top of the larger one.
4. Using permanent markers, write the lowercase letters on the smaller circle and the uppercase letters on the larger circle. Make sure to turn the wheel as you write the letters so that the letters on both wheels match.
5. Make additional wheels for a small group of children to use.

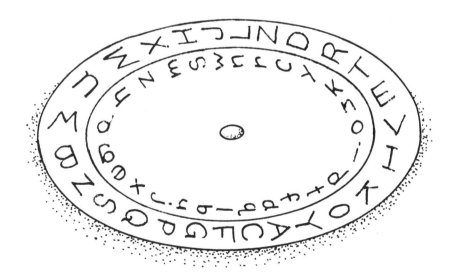

How to Play:

1. Give each child a lid wheel. Begin the game by asking the children to find a letter on their wheels. For example: "Can you find the letter Ww?"
2. The children can take turns asking others in the group to find a letter.
3. Play continues for a predetermined time or until each child has had a specified number of turns.

Other Ideas!

You can make lid wheels to cover most skills you want to reinforce. Children can work with the wheels to match shapes, numbers, colors, or any other readiness skills. Perhaps the children in your class-room need additional practice with concepts such as rhyming words, opposites, or identifying word parts (phonemic awareness).

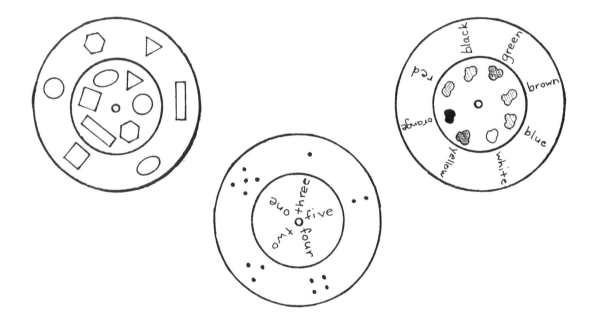

GO FISH!

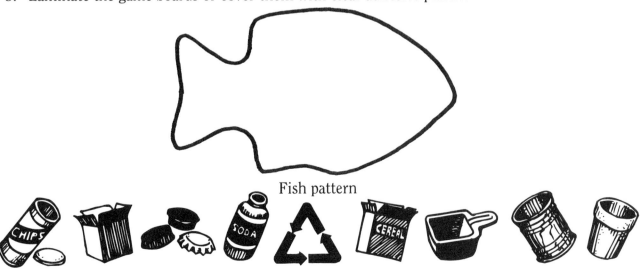

Skill:
Capital and lowercase letters/sight words

Materials Needed:
- clear adhesive plastic or laminating material
- craft knife
- pattern page 35
- permanent marker
- several Styrofoam meat trays
- small fish net (used for goldfish or tropical fish)
- small tub with water

Directions for Assembly:
1. Using the pattern below, trace and cut out 27 fish from Styrofoam trays.
2. With a permanent marker, write capital letters or sight words on the fish, one on each fish. If the children are practicing sight words, select words that are appropriate. Here are some common sight words:

am	can	find	help	look	play	three
and	cat	funny	here	me	please	two
are	come	girls	is	my	red	up
at	did	go	it	not	run	want
away	do	good	jump	off	said	was
big	dog	happy	like	on	see	we
boys	down	have	little	one	the	you

3. Duplicate three copies of the game board pattern and mount them on construction paper.
4. Prepare the game boards by printing the lowercase letters on the fish or print different sight words on each board (words from the list of 27 sight words you have chosen to use).
5. Laminate the game boards or cover them with clear adhesive plastic.

Fish pattern

How to Play:

1. Place the Styrofoam fish in a small tub of water.
2. Encourage two or three children to play the game.
3. Each student selects a game board and then takes a turn using the net to "catch" a fish.
4. Have the player name the fish which is caught and then try to find the matching fish on his/her game board. Place the Styrofoam fish on the corresponding shape. If the letter/word is not found on the game board, have the player return the fish to the "pond."
5. Play continues until all fish have been caught or until one game board is filled.

Other Ideas!

Of course many skills can be practiced with this type of game—matching math facts with answers, identifying color words, and so on. Just think about what is happening in your classroom and make the game accordingly.

MATCH THE KEY

Skill:
Beginning consonant sounds or blends

Materials Needed:
- assorted old keys or plastic baby keys (baby's rattle)
- clear adhesive plastic
- craft knife
- pattern page 37–39 or pictures from old workbooks and catalogs
- permanent markers
- shoe box

Directions for Assembly:

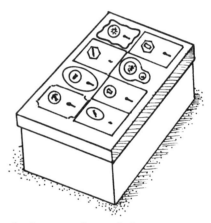

1. Make a copy of the pattern page (choose either beginning consonant sounds or blends) and mount it on the lid of your shoe box. Color the pictures as desired. Cover the lid of your shoe box with contact paper. *Note:* You may prefer to use pictures that you have collected from magazines, old workbooks and catalogs. Mount those pictures instead of the pattern page on the box lid.
2. Using the craft knife, cut enough slits in the lid to match the number of pictures.
3. With a permanent marker, write the corresponding letter or letters for the beginning sound of each of the picture on a key.
4. Store the game keys inside the shoe box.

How to Play:
1. Place the game in an area where it can be used by children as a center activity or as an optional activity when work is completed.
2. The child places the keys into the appropriate slits.

Other Ideas!
Be sure to collect and prepare several lids that match the same shoe box base. It is easy to locate additional pictures that match the set of beginning sound keys or blends keys you have already made. This game also works well for reviewing final consonant sounds or long vowel sounds. Just follow the same directions for assembling the games as you glue or draw pictures to represent those sounds.

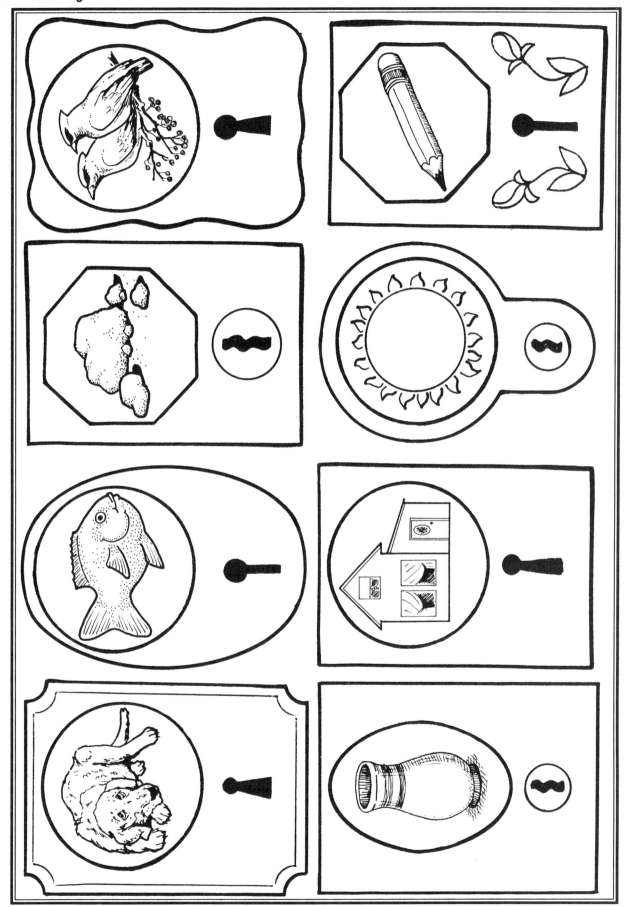

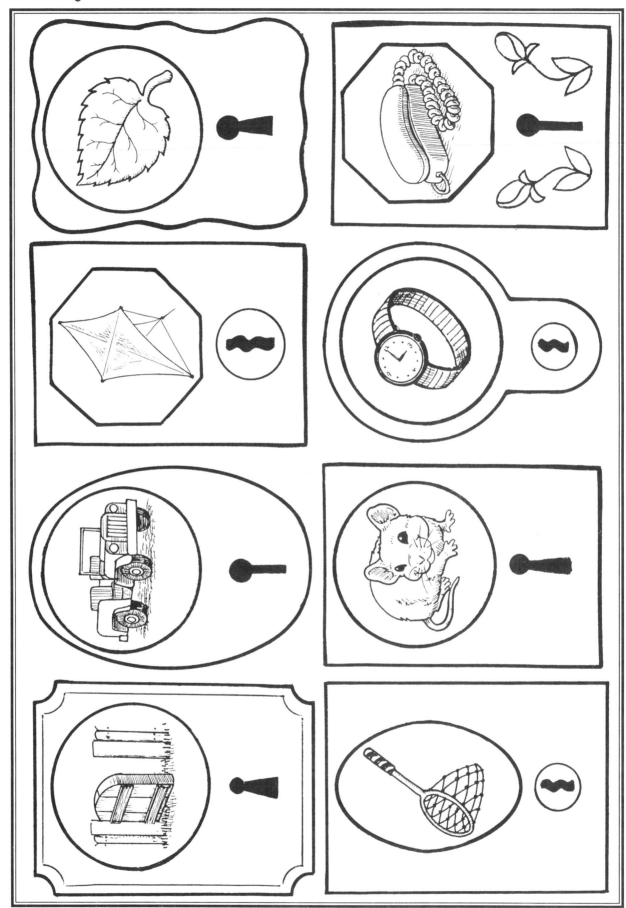

Match the Key Pattern-Blends

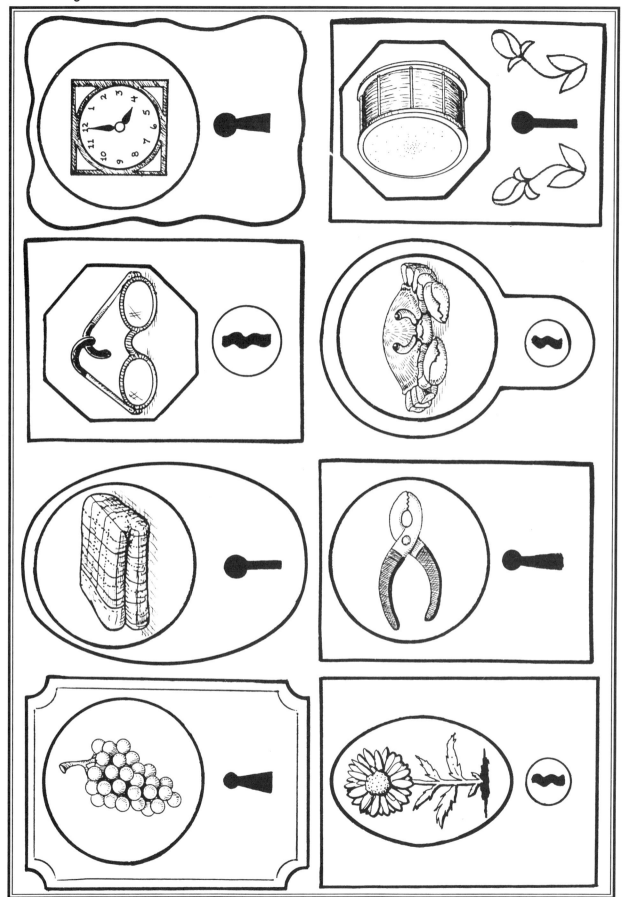

THREE IN A ROW BINGO

Skill:

Beginning consonant sounds—Bb, Cc, Dd, Ff, Gg, Hh, Jj, Kk, Ll, Mm, Nn, Pp, Qq, Rr, Ss, Tt, Vv, Ww, Yy, and Zz

Language Arts

Materials Needed:

- bingo markers (pennies, kernels of corn, buttons, small paper squares, or any other small item)
- clear adhesive plastic or laminating material
- construction paper
- one EMPTY sticker backing sheet for each player (no stickers on sheet—three spaces across and three spaces down)
- pattern pages 42–43
- permanent markers
- ruler
- scissors
- small can or box

Directions for Assembly:

1. Cut construction paper to match the size of sticker sheets. The sheets are approximately 4½" x 5½" (115 x 140 mm). Cut enough so that there is one for each sticker sheet.
2. Separate the sticker sheet from the backing card and mount the frame on the construction paper. This will the bingo game board. The bingo spaces are the empty sticker spaces.
3. Using a permanent marker, write a consonant letter in each space in random order. If you wish to concentrate on certain letters, display only those letters on your game boards. Please note that you may use the letters more than once because three word cards are provided for each beginning consonant sound.
4. Cover your game boards with clear adhesive plastic or laminate them for durability.
5. Photocopy the word cards on pages 42-43. Laminate the copies, then cut apart the word cards. Place them in a can or box for drawing.

How to Play:

1. Select a small group of children to play. You may choose to make enough game boards to play the game with a large group.
2. Have the children sit with their game boards and a small pile of markers in front of them.
3. Draw a word card and read it.
4. Each player identifies the beginning sound and places a marker on the corresponding letter if it is shown on her/his game board.
5. Play continues until a child calls out "Three in a Row!"
6. Use the discarded word cards to check the child's game board.
7. If the game board is filled correctly, have all the players empty their game boards and begin a new game.
8. If the game board is filled incorrectly, remove the incorrect game markers and then continue the game until someone is the winner.

Other Ideas!

Make the game boards in the same way but change the skill to reinforce other concepts: recognizing color words, alphabet letters, number words, final consonant sounds, and much, much more.

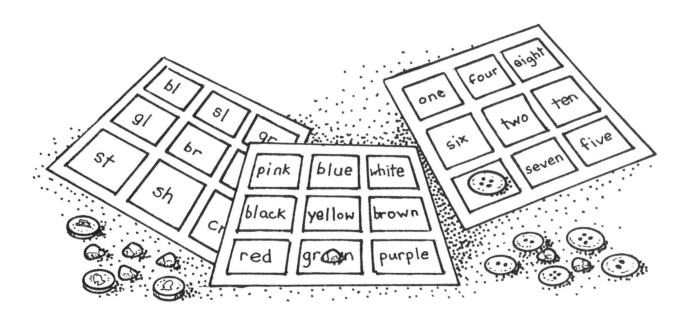

bat	baby	bed
cake	corn	candle
dog	door	doll
foot	five	flag
gate	girl	goat
hat	hand	hammer
jeep	jacks	jail
kite	king	key
leaf	lion	lamp
mitten	man	mop

nest	name	numbers
pig	pencil	pipe
question	quail	quilt
rake	ring	rug
seven	star	sign
toast	time	train
volcano	vest	violin
worm	wagon	watch
yo-yo	yolk	yarn
zero	zoo	zebra

"X" MARKS THE SPOT

Language Arts

Skill:
Beginning consonant sounds

Materials Needed:
- ¼" (6 mm) floor tile spacers
  (available at hardware or lumber stores)
- clear adhesive plastic or laminating material
- pattern pages 45–50
- permanent and watercolor markers
- scissors
- small colored dots in red, blue, and green
- three colorful file folders
- three resealable plastic bags

Directions for Assembly:
1. Photocopy the game board patterns on pages 45–50. Decorate with watercolor markers, cut out, and mount them on colorful file folders.
2. Cover the game boards with clear adhesive plastic or laminate them.
3. With a permanent marker, write the following letters on the floor tile spacers: Game A–letters B, K, P, V, H, R, W; Game B–letters C, D, J, N, Z, F, M; Game C–letters Q, T, G, L, S, Y, B.
4. In order to keep the game pieces organized, color code them. Place a red dot on the back of each letter piece for Game A and a matching red dot on the game board. Place a blue dot on each component for Game B and green dots on all Game C pieces.
5. Place game pieces in resealable plastic bags.

How to Play:
1. Ask three children to play the game.
2. Give each player a game board and matching game pieces.
3. Have each child follow the path and place the corresponding letter near the picture.
4. When each player is finished, clear the boards and rotate the games between the children.

Other Ideas!
Using the blank game board on pages 51–52, create your own games. Other possibilities are counting games (draw different sets in the treasure boxes and write the numerals on the tile spaces), capital and lowercase letter match, final consonant sounds, word families (cat, bat for "at"), vowel sounds, basic math facts. Be creative, there are many variations for this game!

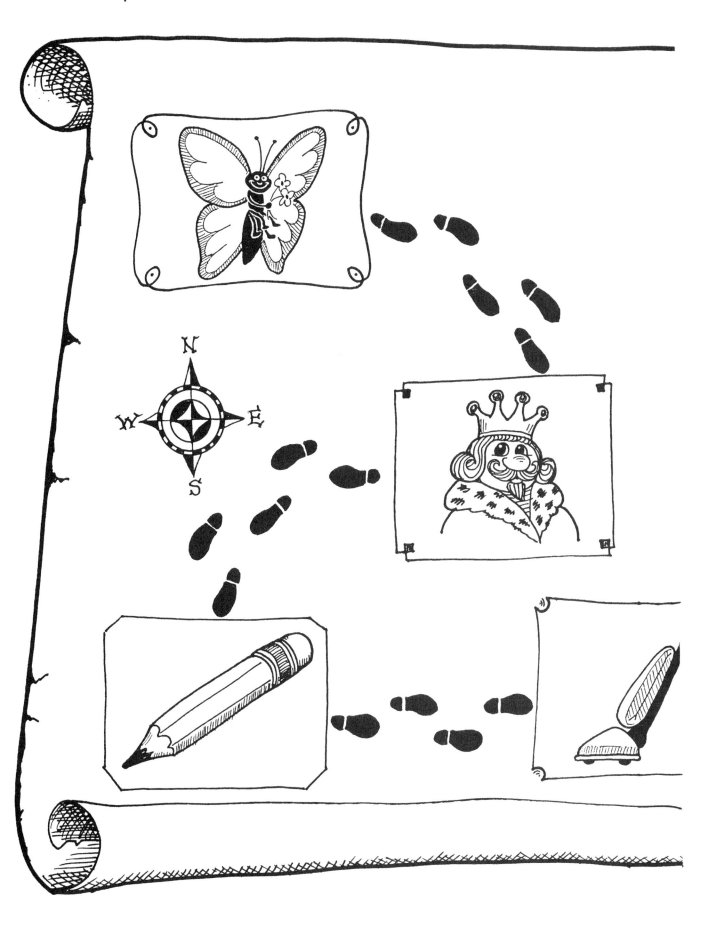

45

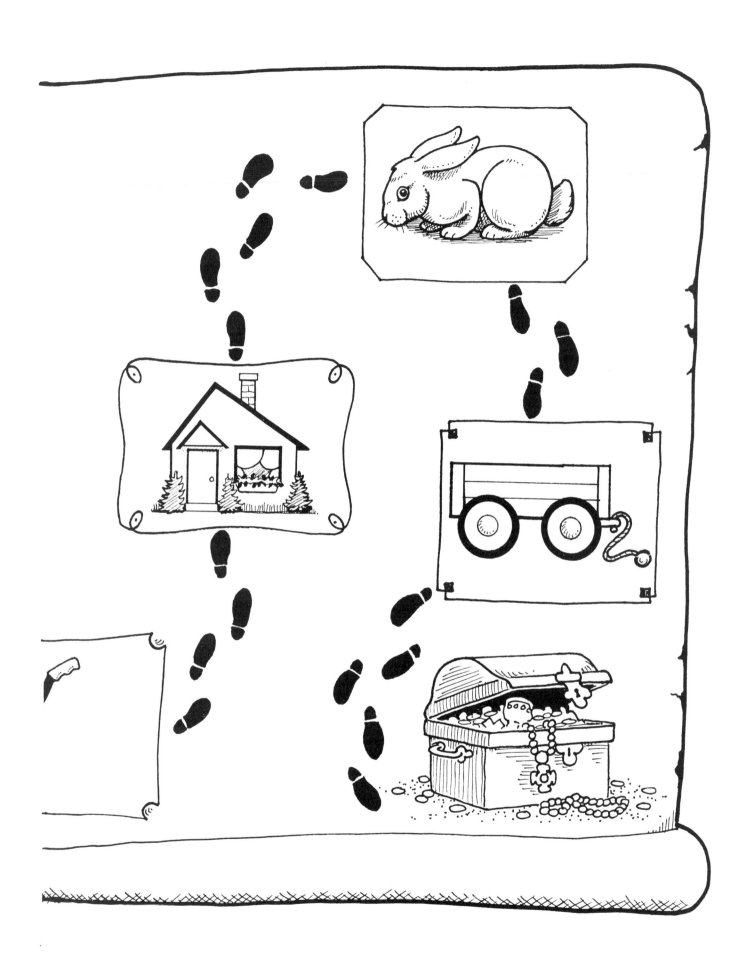

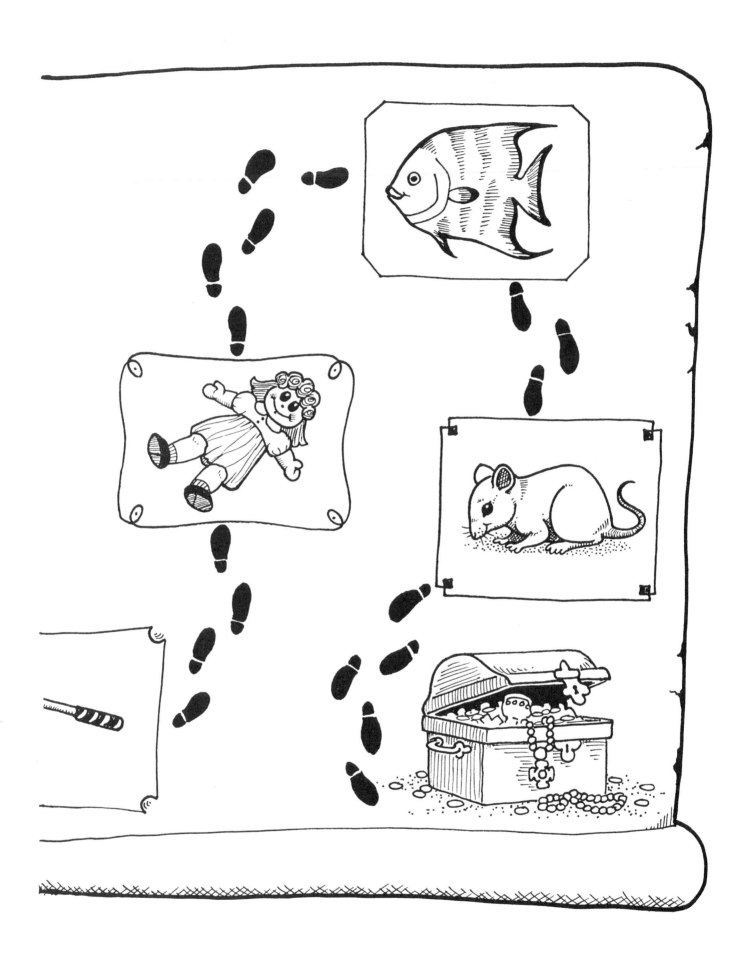

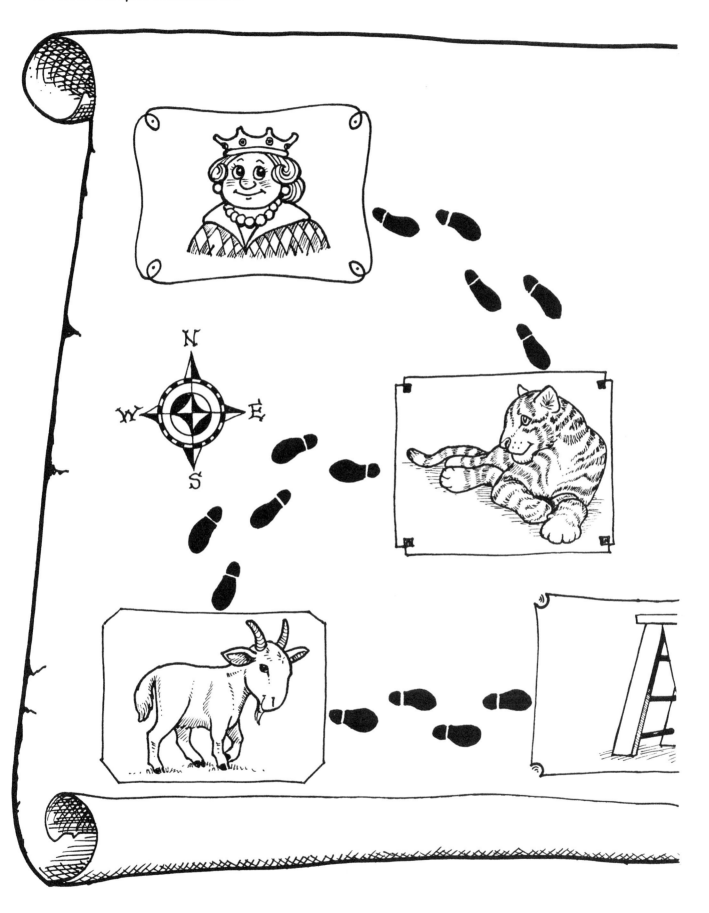

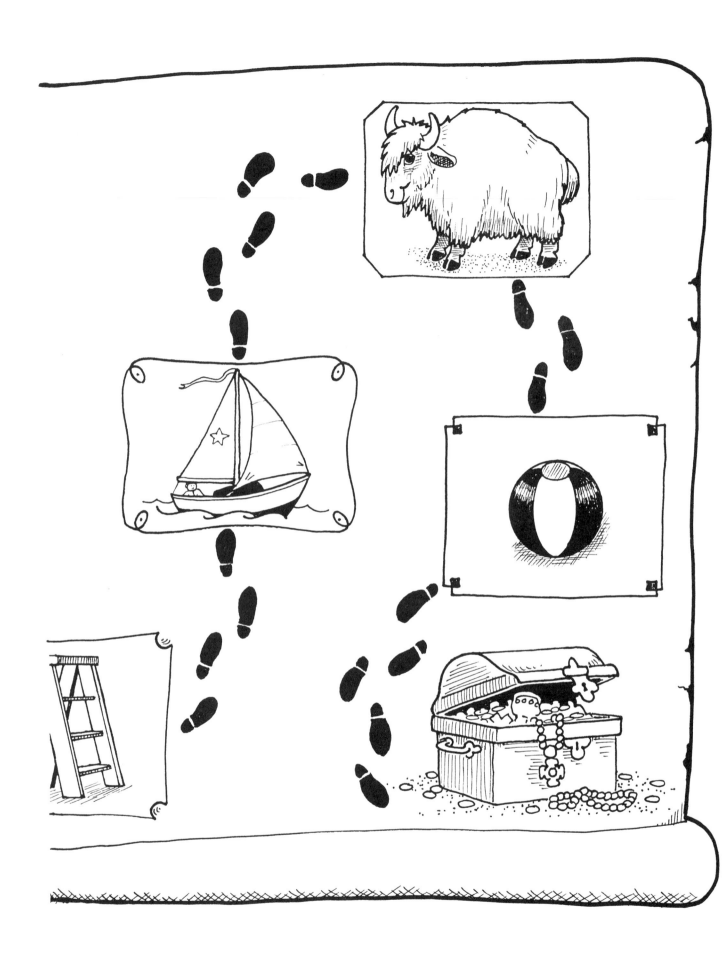

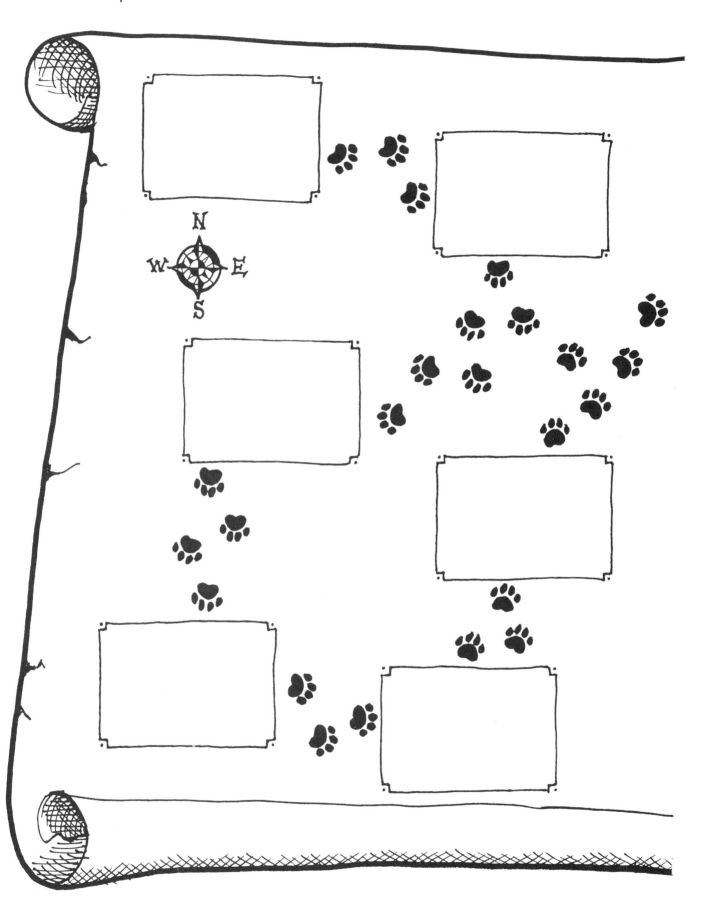

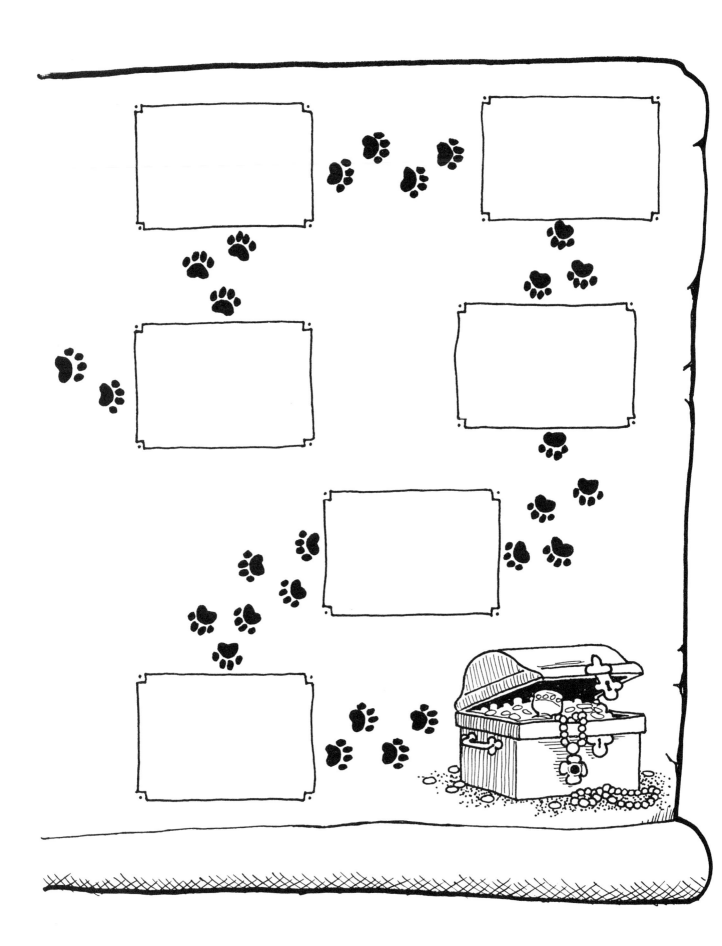

HANG THE LAUNDRY

Language Arts

Skill:
Rhyming words

Materials Needed:
- hole punch
- clear adhesive plastic or laminating material
- nine plastic hooks found on socks or kitchen towels when displayed in store
- one empty ribbon cardboard roll
- pattern pages 54–62
- scissors
- small berry basket for the "laundry"
- suction cup hooks (optional)
- various colors of construction paper
- 6 feet (183 cm) yarn or string

Directions for Assembly:
1. Begin stringing the sock hooks onto the string, tying a knot before and after the hook to secure it. Allow 3 or 4 inches (76 or 102 mm) between each sock hook and 12 inches (305 mm) at either end. Cut any remaining string off and make a small loop at each end.
2. Wind your sock hook clothesline onto the empty ribbon roll for storage.
3. Photocopy the patterns for the laundry onto construction paper using several colors for variety.
4. Laminate the pieces or cover them with clear adhesive plastic for durability.
5. Punch a hole in the top of each piece of laundry so that it can easily be hung from a plastic hook.

How to Play:

1. Hang the clothesline from small suction cup hooks or by simply taping the ends to the wall or a window, making sure it is accessible to the children.
2. Place the "laundry" in a basket next to the clothesline in the center.
3. Working in pairs, let the children find the matching rhymes and then hang them on the clothesline by placing a matching pair on each hook.

Other Ideas!
To make the game easier for the children, hang one piece of each pair on a hook before playing. The children then find the matching piece and hang it. This can also be a self-checking activity; identical stickers, colored dots, or numbers can be placed on the back of each matching pair of laundry.

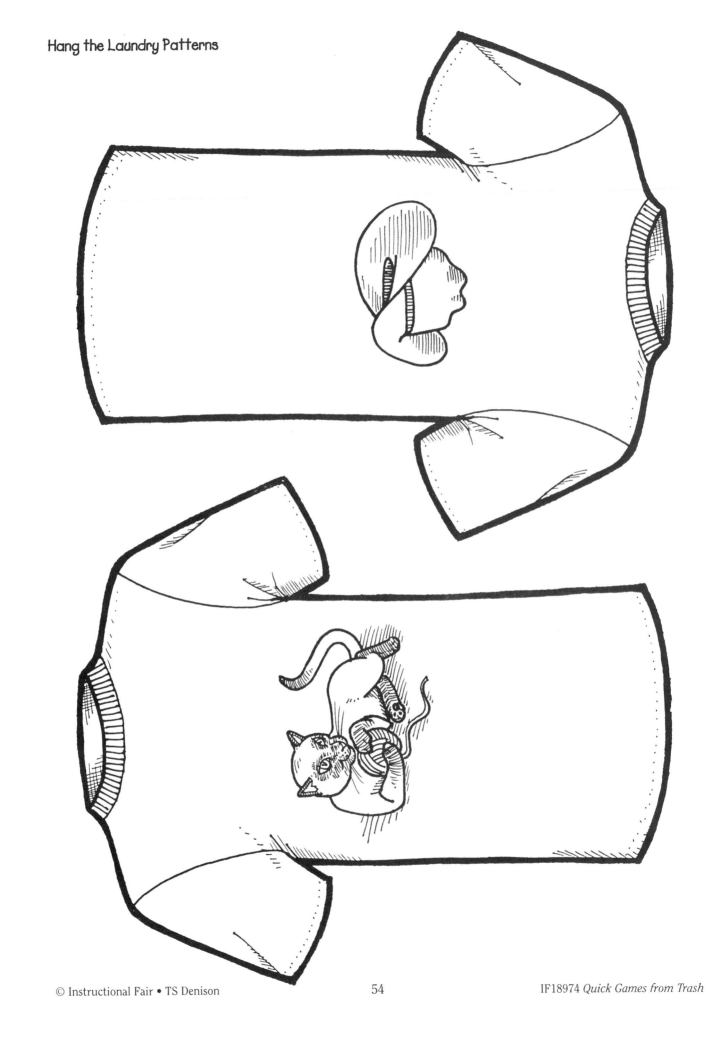

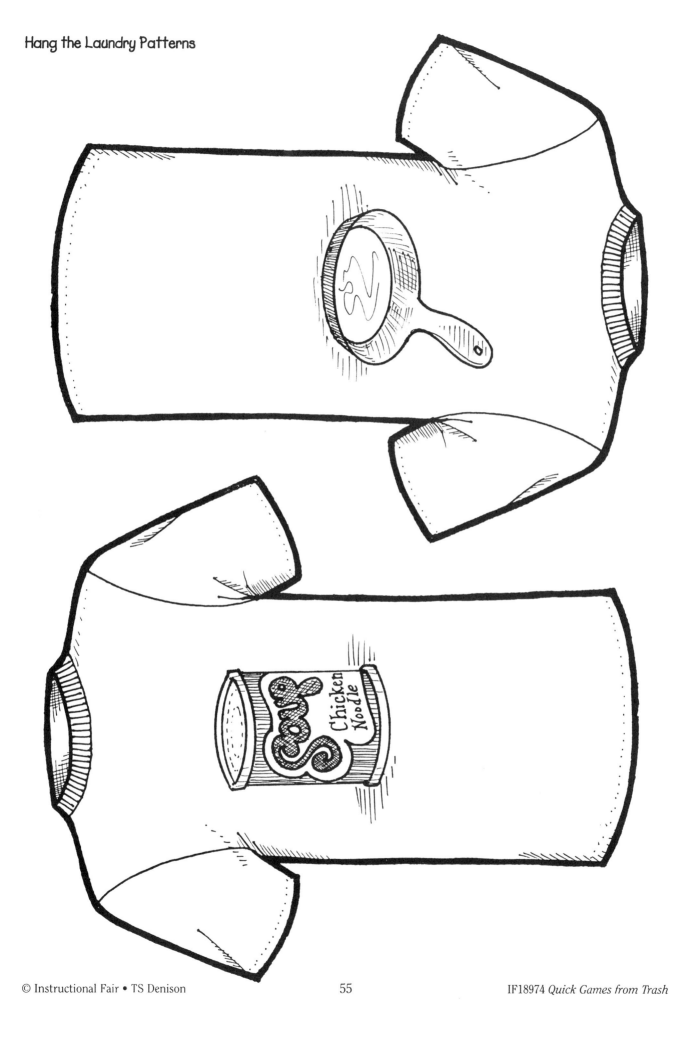

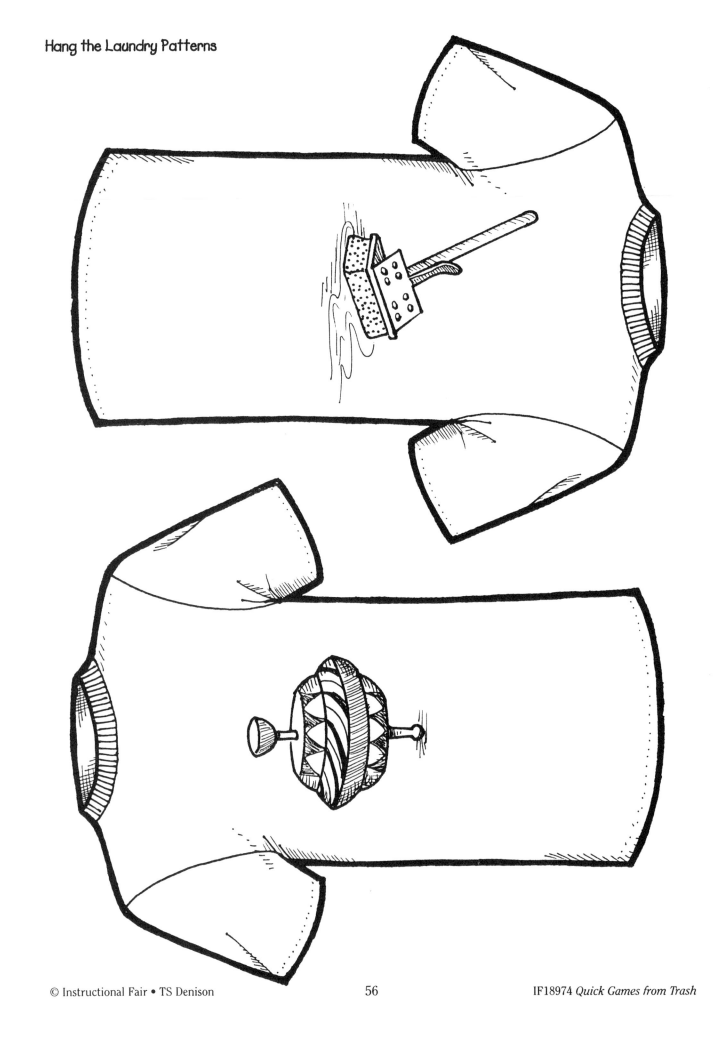

Hang the Laundry Patterns

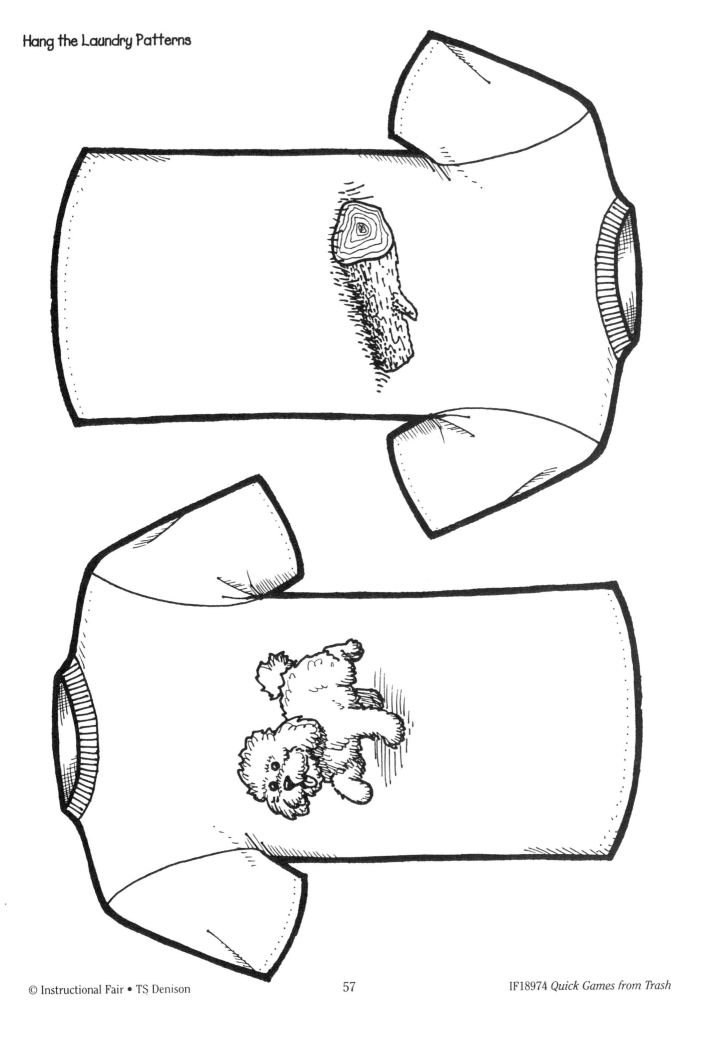

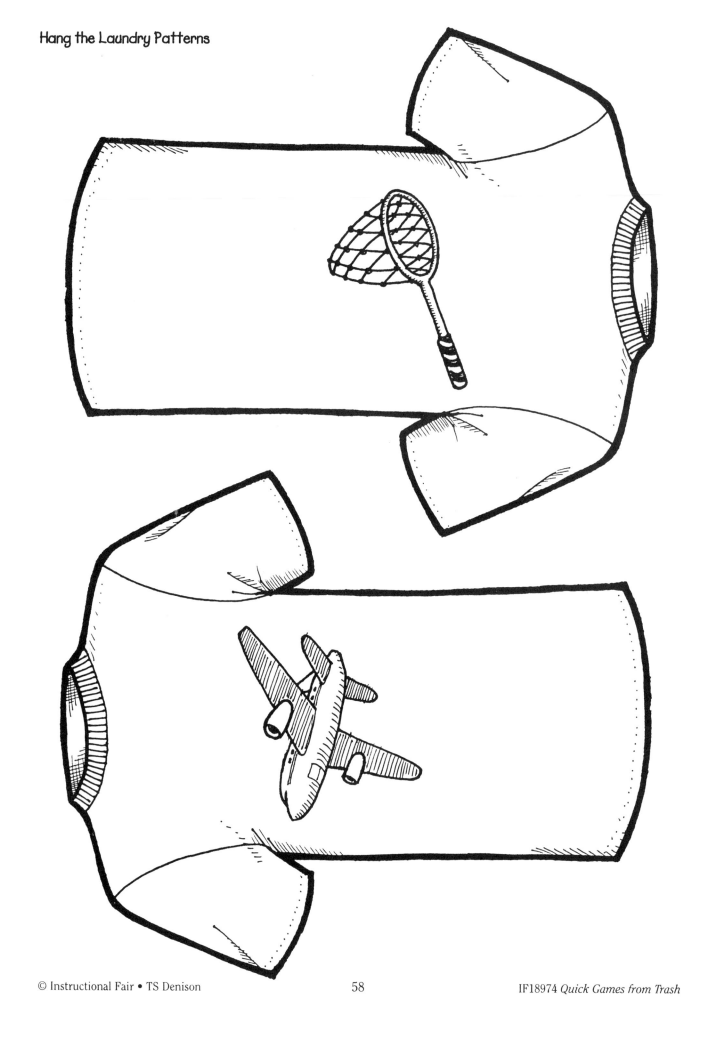

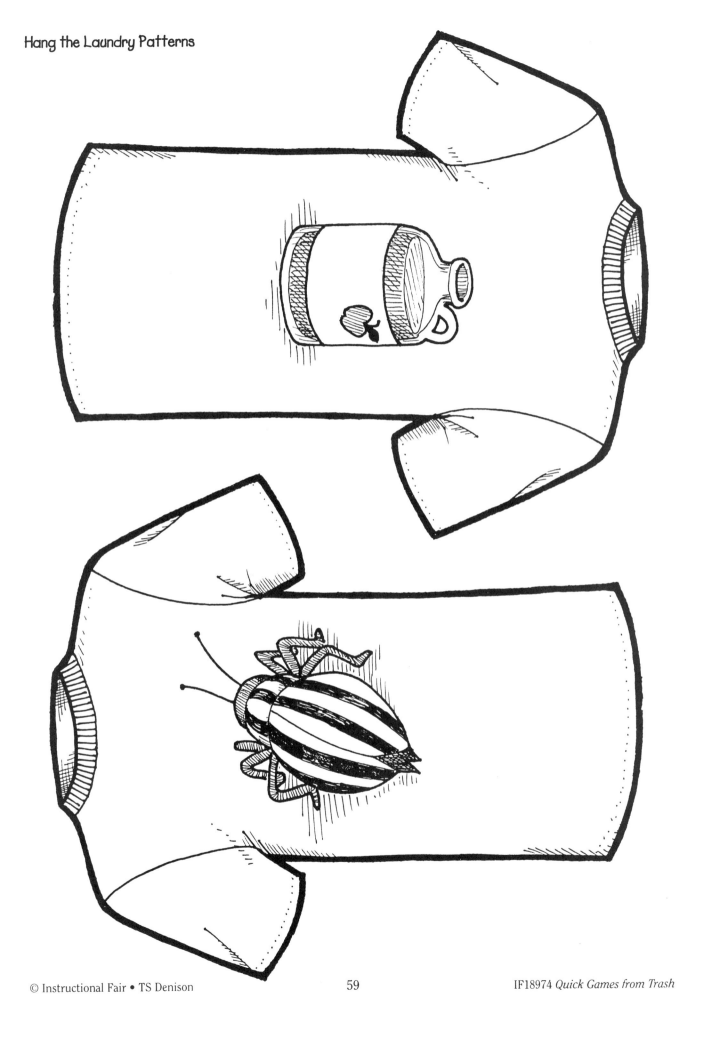

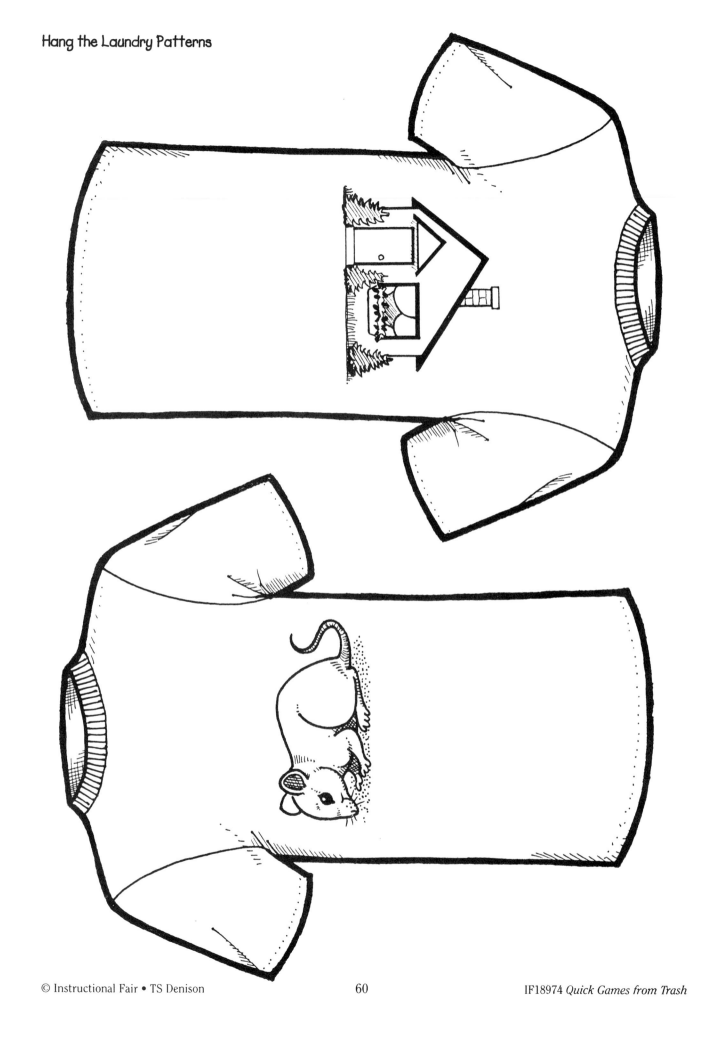

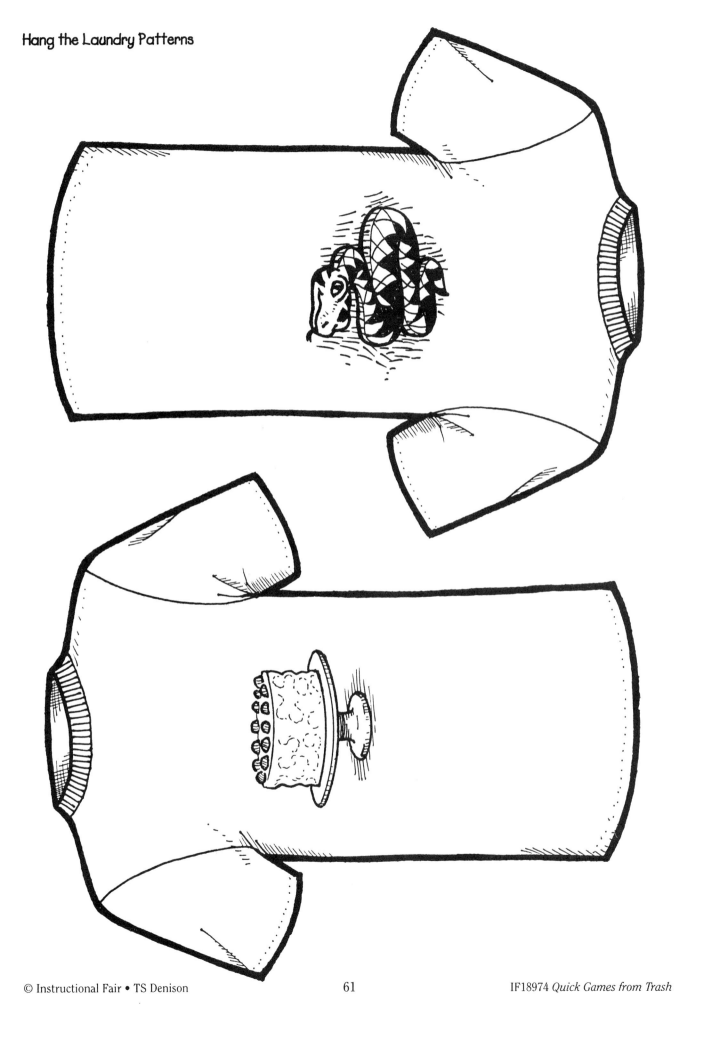

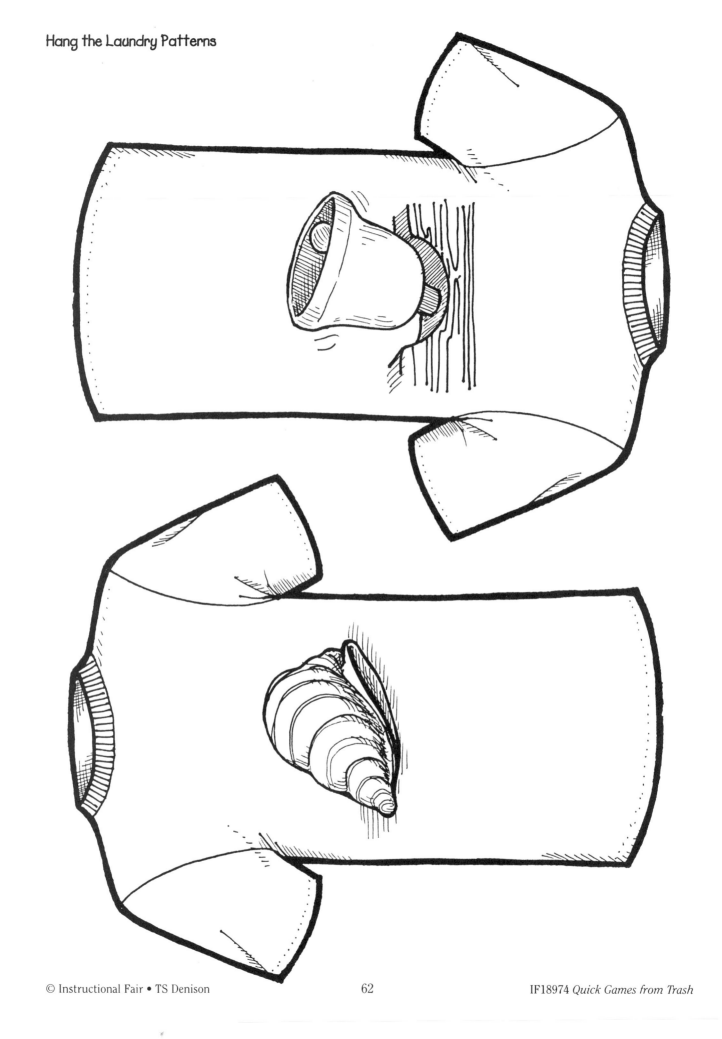

RING IT!

Skill:
Rhyming words

Materials Needed:
- clear adhesive plastic or laminating material
- four sheets of construction paper, each a different color
- pattern pages 64–67
- plastic rings from the top of gallon (37.8 ml) milk containers with screw type lids, ten rings per game board
- resealable plastic bag or small container

Directions for Assembly:
1. Copy the game board patterns onto colored construction, making each game board a different color.
2. Laminate the game boards or cover them with clear adhesive plastic for durability.
3. Collect the plastic rings from milk jugs which have screw type lids that separate from the rings. Just pull the ring off the empty container and save. Place the rings in the plastic bag or container and store them with the game boards.

How to Play:
1. Select a small group of three or four children to play the game or place the game pieces in a center for individual use.
2. Have the children place the rings around matching rhyming pairs in each row.
3. When finished, the children may exchange game boards for additional practice. The game ends when all rhyming pairs are found.

Other Ideas!
Use the rings in a variety of ways. There are many activities that require children to use grease pencils to circle answers. Children can easily finish the activity by using rings and then quickly clear the activity boards. Another plus, you can check at a glance to see if the activity has been completed correctly. Additional task cards are easy to make; convert old workbook pages or worksheets by laminating them and providing milk jug rings for the children to use in centers.

Ring It!

Ring It!

Ring It!

Ring It!

LIGHTBULB MATCH

Language Arts

Skill:
Opposites (Antonyms)

Materials Needed:
- clear adhesive plastic or laminating material
- one empty lightbulb box (60 watts)
- patterns on pages 69–73
- scissors
- small stickers or watercolor markers
- yellow paper

Directions for Assembly:
1. Copy the lightbulb patterns onto yellow paper.
2. If you wish to make the game self-checking, adhere identical stickers or draw small colored dots with markers on the back of each pair of matching lightbulbs.
3. Cover the lightbulbs with clear adhesive plastic or laminate them for durability.
4. Cut out the lightbulbs before storing them in the empty lightbulb box.

How to Play:
1. Place the lightbulbs in front of a small group of children, making sure they can all see the pictures.
2. Taking turns, have the children try to find pairs that have opposite meanings.
3. If the game is self-checking, the children can check their selections by turning over the pairs of cards to see if they have identical markings or stickers. If the cards do not match, return the cards to the playing area.
4. Play continues until all pairs have been identified.

Other Ideas!
The children can also play a memory game with the cards. For "Lightbulb Memory Match" provide a set of cards *without* stickers or colored dots on the backs. Let two or three children play the game. To begin play, arrange the cards *face down* in rows or in random fashion. The first player selects two cards and turns them *face up*. If the lightbulbs are the correct pair, the child keeps the lightbulbs. If the lightbulbs do not show pictures that have opposite meanings, the child returns them *face down*. The next player repeats the process. Play continues until all correct pairs have been found. *Optional:* The child with the most pairs of cards is the winner.

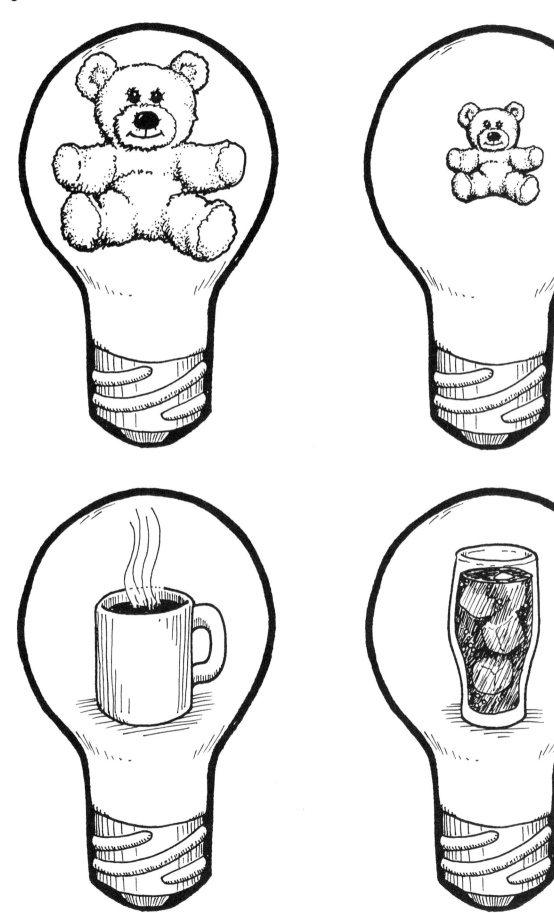

Lightbulb Match Patterns

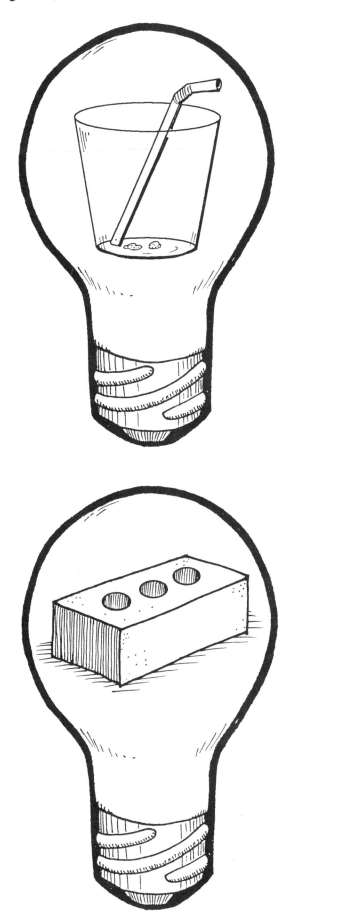

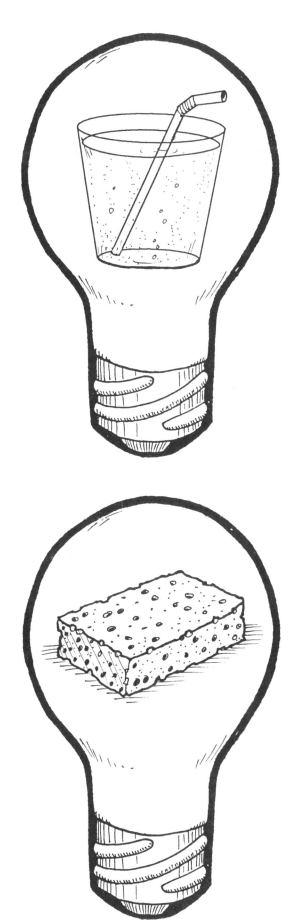

Lightbulb Match Patterns

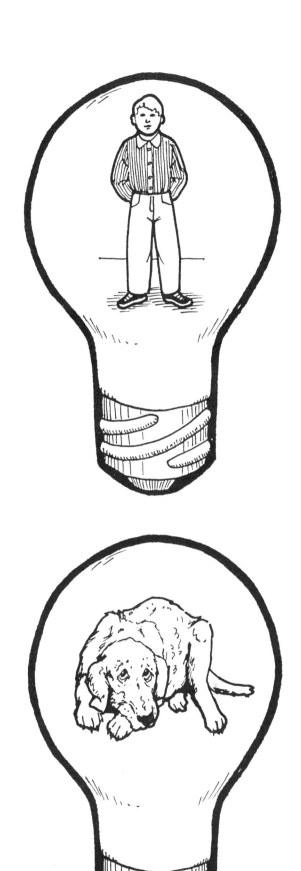

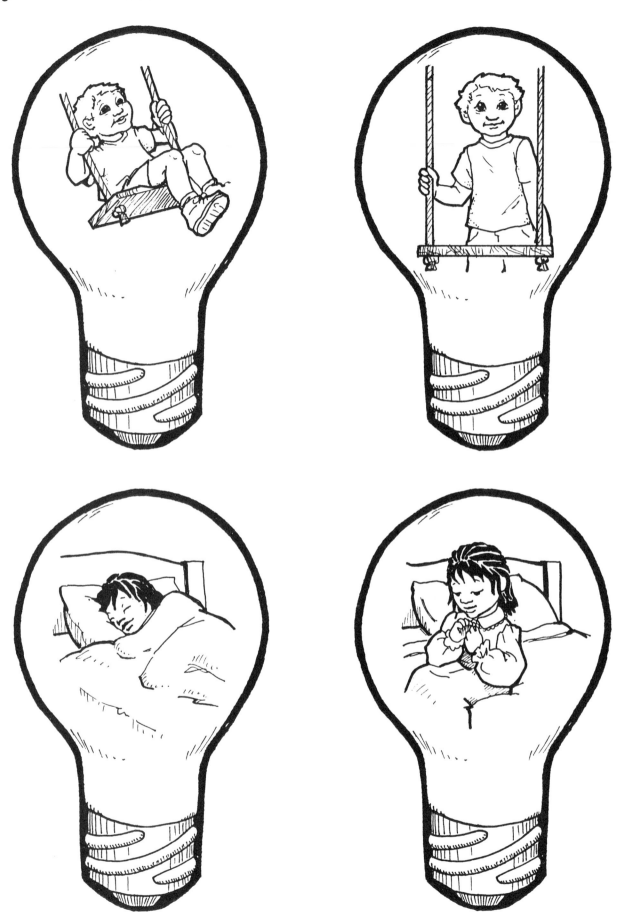

Lightbulb Match Patterns

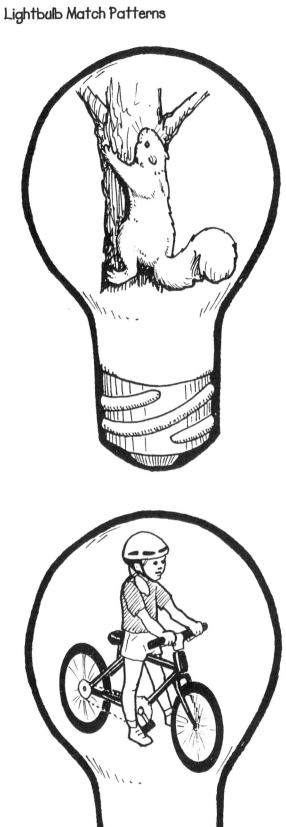

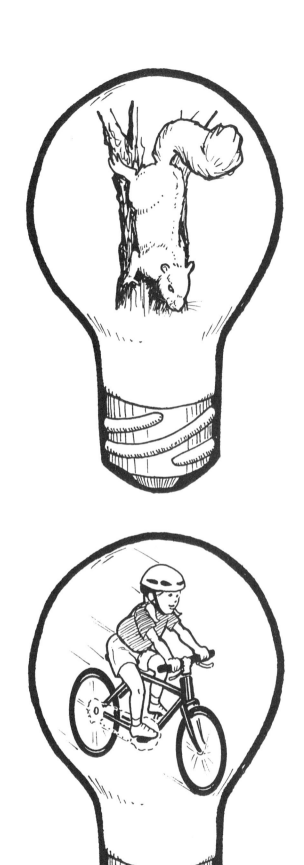

THE YOLK SAYS

Skill:
Opposites

Language Arts

Materials Needed:
- 12 plastic eggs (available before the Easter holiday)
- glue
- laminating material
- one empty egg carton
- patterns on pages 75–79
- scissors
- two colorful file folders
- white construction paper
- watercolor markers

Directions for Assembly:
1. Copy the patterns for the eggs from pages 75–76 onto white construction paper.
2. With the yellow marker, color the center circle of each egg yellow to make a yolk.
3. Laminate the eggs for durability.
4. Cut out the eggs and place one inside each plastic egg. Place the eggs in the egg carton.
5. Photocopy pattern pages 77–79 on brown construction paper for the game board. Color as desired.
6. Staple the two folders together to make three panels for the game board. Mount the game board copies according to the illustration.
7. Laminate the folder for durability.

How to Play:
1. Invite two or three children to play the game.
2. Place the game board in the middle of the group.
3. Pass the egg carton to the first child. That child selects an egg and "cracks" it, removing the game piece.
4. The child finds the matching opposite on the frying pan and places the egg on top.
5. Play continues until all of the eggs have been placed on the correct frying pans.

Other Ideas!
This game can be used by a child working individually in a center or as a circle activity, during which time one child "cracks" the egg and another child locates the matching frying pan.

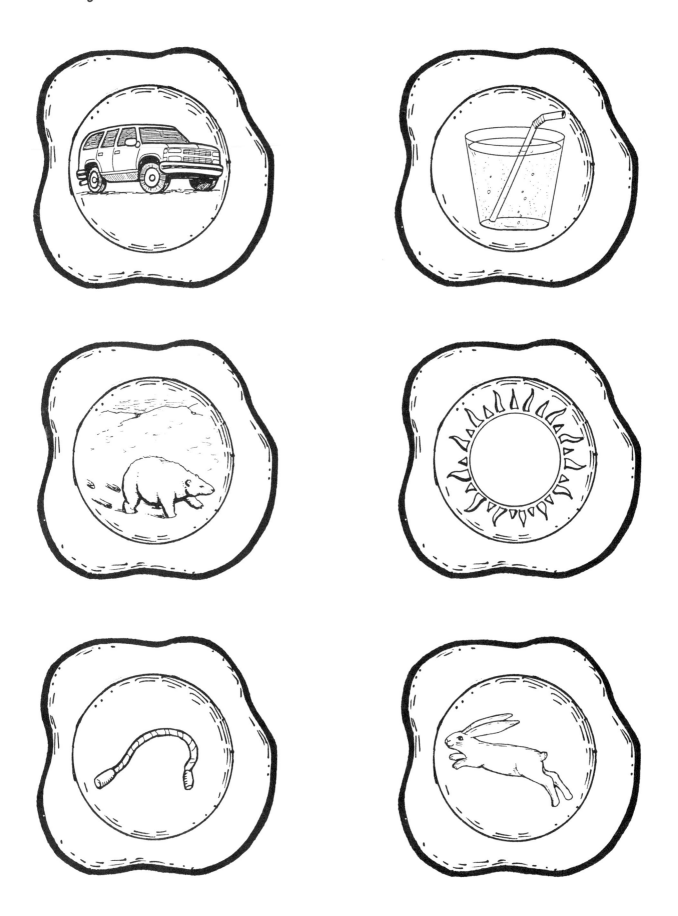

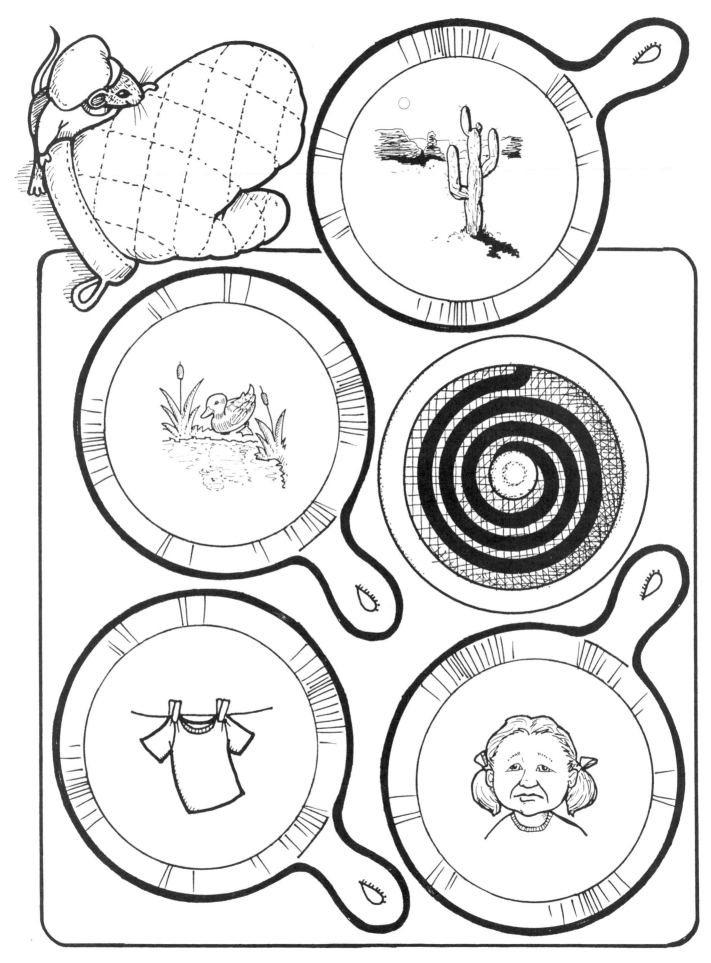

79

BOO HOO!

Skill:
Color and number word recognition/sight words

Materials Needed:
- clear adhesive plastic or laminating material
- one empty facial tissue box
- pattern pages 81–84
- permanent marker
- scissors
- timer
- white construction paper

Directions for Assembly:
1. Photocopy patterns onto construction paper. To make your own playing cards, print sight words on copies of the blank pattern page.
2. Cover the copies with clear adhesive plastic or laminate them.
3. Cut out each face and place it inside the facial tissue box.
4. Write "Boo Hoo" on the outside of the tissue box with the permanent marker.

How to Play:
1. Invite two to four children to play the game.
2. Set the timer for a short amount of time.
3. The first player begins by drawing a face from the box and then reads the word.
4. If the word is read correctly, the player places the face near him and passes the box to the next player. If the word is incorrectly read, the card is returned to the box.
5. When a player draws a "Boo Hoo" face, the turn is forfeited and the box is passed to the next player.
6. Play continues until the timer rings. *Optional:* The children may count their earned faces to determine a winner.

Other Ideas!
Change the skill on the faces to reinforce an appropriate skill for your classroom. The children may work on color recognition, practice basic math facts, and so on. Use the blank pattern page (see page 84) to create the game cards.

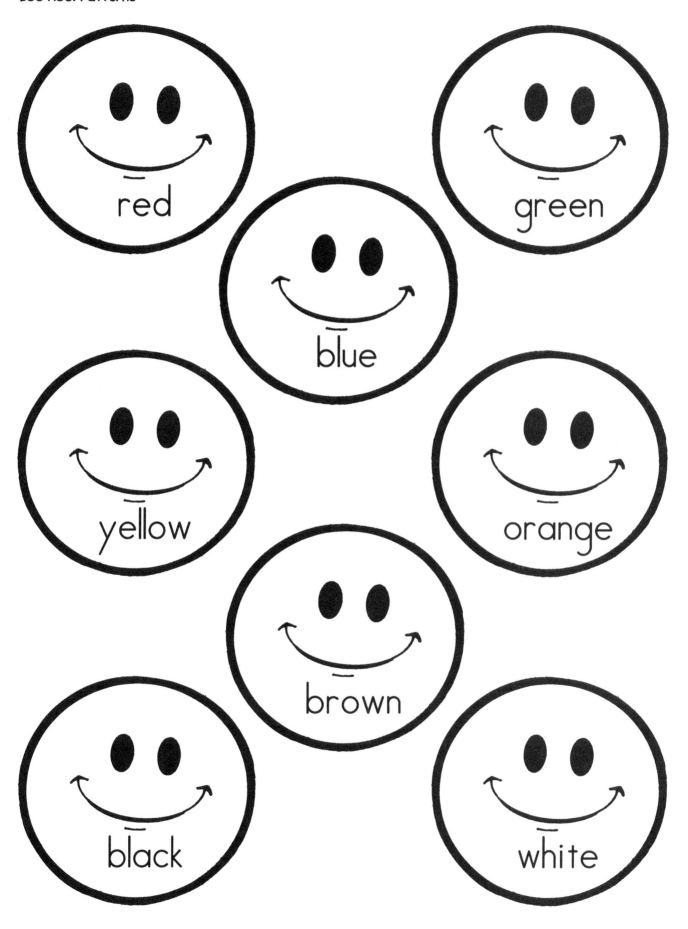

seven

eight

nine

ten

Boo Hoo

Boo Hoo

Boo Hoo

Boo Hoo

Boo Hoo

Boo Hoo

Boo Hoo

LITTLE MOUSE, LITTLE MOUSE, FIND YOUR HOUSE!

Language Arts

Skill:
Recognizing color words

Materials Needed:
- clear adhesive plastic or laminating material
- empty canister or potato chip can with lid
- four sheets of gray construction paper
- glue
- one sheet of construction paper in each color: red, yellow, blue, green, orange, black, brown, white, purple, pink
- pattern pages 87–89
- ruler
- scissors and craft knife
- ten empty cereal boxes (14–16 ounces or 392–448 grams)
- yarn for mice tails

Directions for Assembly:
1. Using a ruler, measure 5" (127 mm) from the bottom and cut off the extra height on the back and the sides of the cereal boxes as shown.
2. Photocopy the pattern of the house in each color (enlarge if necessary to fit on the front of the cereal box) and then glue them to the front of the cereal boxes.
3. Using the craft knife cut along the roof line to remove the top portion of the cereal box panel. When finished, the box will show the outline of the house.
4. Reproduce two copies of the mice pattern pages on gray construction paper.
5. Cut out the mice and then laminate them for durability.
6. To make the tail, glue a small piece of yarn on each mouse.
7. Store the mice in a canister. *Note:* You will have two mice for each color word.

How to Play:

1. For this game have two to four children gather around the colorful houses.
2. The first player draws one mouse from the container.
3. After reading the color word shown on the mouse, the player finds the matching house and places the mouse inside of it. The second player continues in the same manner.
4. Play continues until all mice have been placed in corresponding houses.

Other Ideas!

On 3" x 5" (76 x 127 mm) cards write color words or additional sight words you wish to reinforce. Place word cards in the houses. When the player places the mouse in the correct house, she removes the card and correctly identifies the color word or sight word written on it.

Make enough mice for each student in your class. As students arrive in the morning, give each child a mouse to correctly identify by placing in the correct house. Repeat each day until you feel the children have mastered the skill.

Remember you can easily change the game so the mice represent a skill your class needs to review: number words—place numerals on houses, addition/subtraction facts—place answers on the houses, and so on.

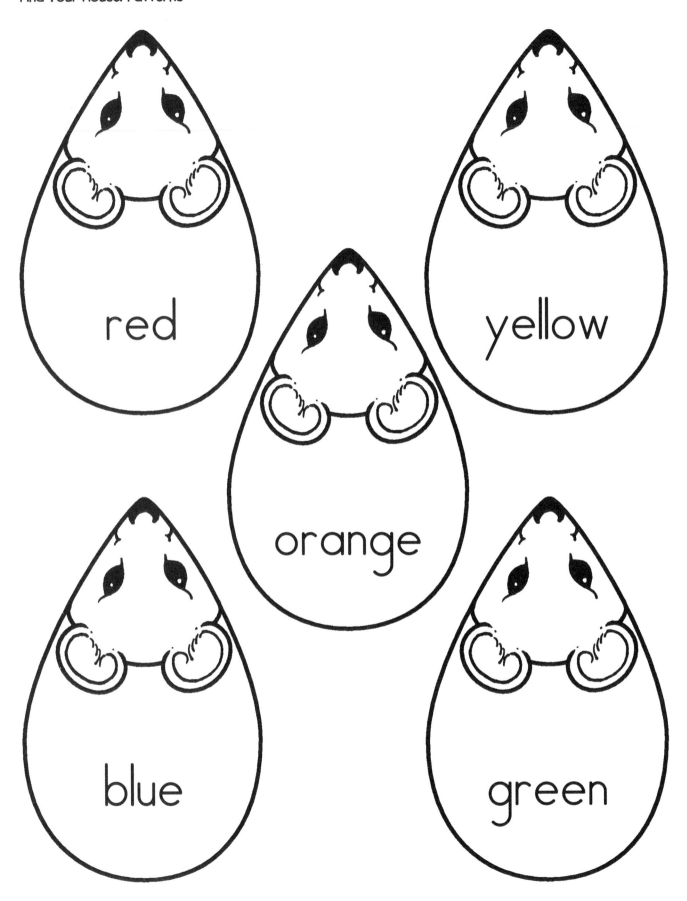

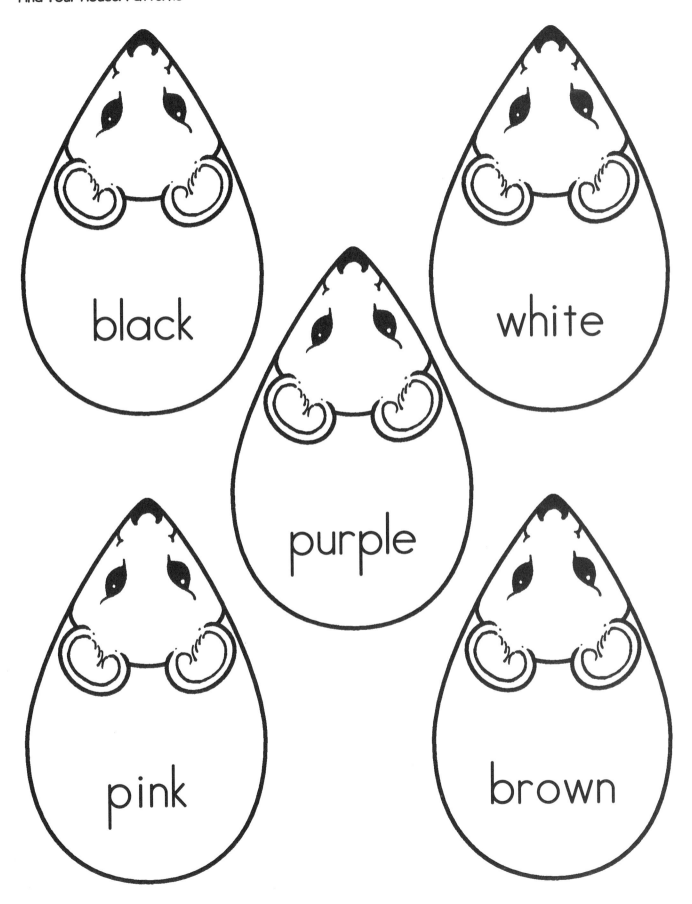

89

WHAT COMES NEXT ON YOUR NECKTIE?

Language Arts

Skill:
Story sequence

Materials Needed:
- clear adhesive plastic or laminating material
- four colors of construction paper
- four men's neckties (discarded or old)
- needle and thread or four large safety pins
- pattern pages 92–95
- Velcro strips
- watercolor markers

Directions for Assembly:
1. Tie each of the neckties into a simple knot. Be sure the loop slips easily over a child's head. See illustration.
2. With the needle and thread make a few simple stitches to secure the knot and prevent it from loosening. If you do not sew, secure the knot with a large safety pin.
3. Place a 1" (25 mm) strip of Velcro (the soft interlocking portion) approximately halfway down the front of each necktie.
4. Photocopy the patterns for the stories and color the scenes. Cut apart the story cards before mounting them on colored construction paper. Be sure to mount each set of four picture cards on different colored construction paper.
5. Cover the pictures with clear adhesive plastic or laminate them for durability.
6. Attach a 1" (25 mm) strip of Velcro (the coarse interlocking portion) to the back of each story card. *Note:* The story cards will be attached to the neckties.

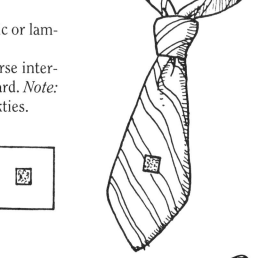

How to Play:

1. Ask four children to wear the neckties.
2. Give the group a set of story cards and have each child attach a card to the necktie.
3. Encourage the children to study the pictures and then figure out what happened first, second, and so on. When the children are ready, ask them to stand in a line and show the correct sequence of events.
4. Continue with another story set until the picture cards for all sets have been successfully placed in order.

Other Ideas!

Play the game as a group. Give four children neckties and one story set. Have them find a quiet place away from the remaining group and work on arranging themselves to show the correct sequence of events. One at a time in the correct order of events they return to the group and tell their part of the story. Repeat with a new group of children and a different set of story cards.

For some children it is easier to work with the cards if the neckties are numbered. To do this, purchase adhesive felt numbers or make your own that can be attached with Velcro pieces. Arrange the cards in numerical order.

Old neckties are easily acquired from parents and other family members. By preparing 16 neckties for this game, four groups of four children can work on sequencing picture cards simultaneously.

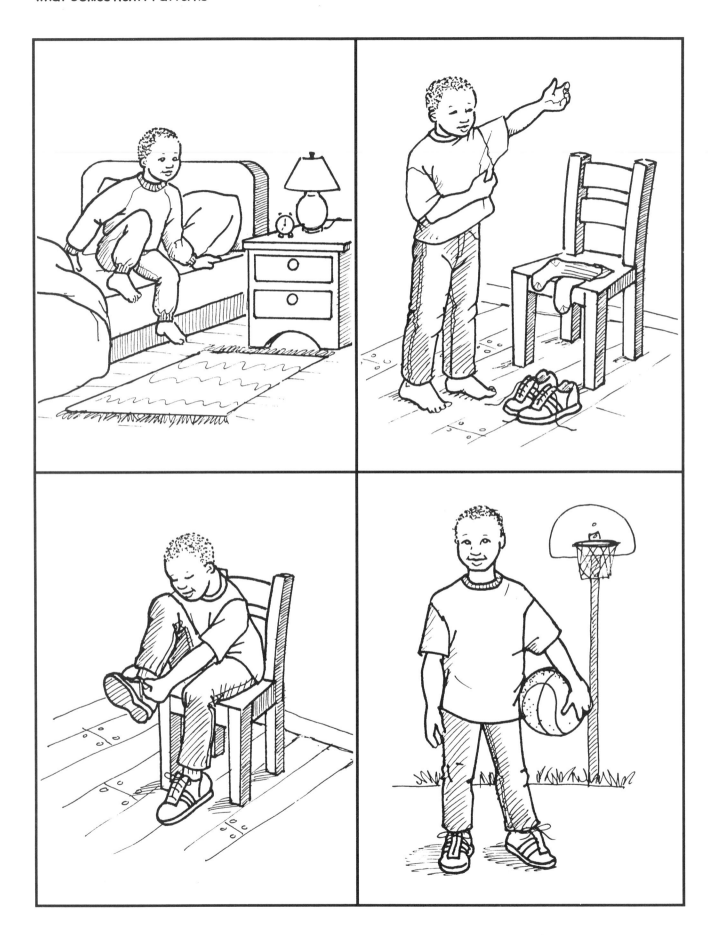

DOTS ON SPOT

Language Arts

Skill:
Vowel sounds

Materials Needed:
- 30 white snap-on or screw-on lids (milk or water jugs)
- black, red, green, and blue permanent markers
- clear adhesive plastic or laminating material
- glue
- pattern pages 98–105
- scissors
- three file folders
- three resealable plastic bags
- watercolor markers

Directions for Assembly:
1. Photocopy the pattern pages and then color them as desired. Color the dog, but leave the circles white.
2. Trim the pattern pages and then mount each set on a separate file folder.
3. In the top corner of each folder game, draw a colored dot with a permanent marker. This will indicate which milk jug lids correspond with each game. On the folder for Game A, place a red dot. Draw a green dot on Game B and a blue dot on Game C.
4. Laminate or cover the game board with clear adhesive plastic.
5. Prepare the game pieces, using permanent markers to write the following vowel sound markings on the top of the lids. Be sure to color code the game pieces by using a different colored marker when printing the following letters for each set:

   Game A (red letters), pattern pages 98-99
   Make two plastic lids for each long vowel sound:

   $$\bar{a} \quad \bar{e} \quad \bar{i} \quad \bar{o} \quad \bar{u}$$

   Game B (green letters), pattern pages 100-101
   Make two plastic lids for each short vowel sound:

   $$\breve{a} \quad \breve{e} \quad \breve{i} \quad \breve{o} \quad \breve{u}$$

   Game C (blue letters), pattern pages 102-103
   Make one lid for each long vowel sound and short vowel sound.
6. Store the game pieces in the plastic bags.

How to Play:

1. Invite a small group of children to play the game.
2. Have the group select a game board.
3. Remove the game pieces from the plastic bag and scatter them in random order around the game board.
4. Point to a picture on the dog. Ask the children to name the picture and then identify the vowel sound which they hear.
5. Find the matching game piece and place it on the dog.
6. Play continues until all of the game pieces have been placed on the game board.
7. Let the children continue the game by working with each game board in the same manner.

Other Ideas!

This activity can be used in a learning center. Place each game board with game pieces in a location where children can play during their free time or at a time designated by the teacher.

Identify other skills or concepts that the children need to practice and then use the blank game board pattern (see pages 104 and 105) to create your "Dots on Spot" game.

Long Vowel Sounds

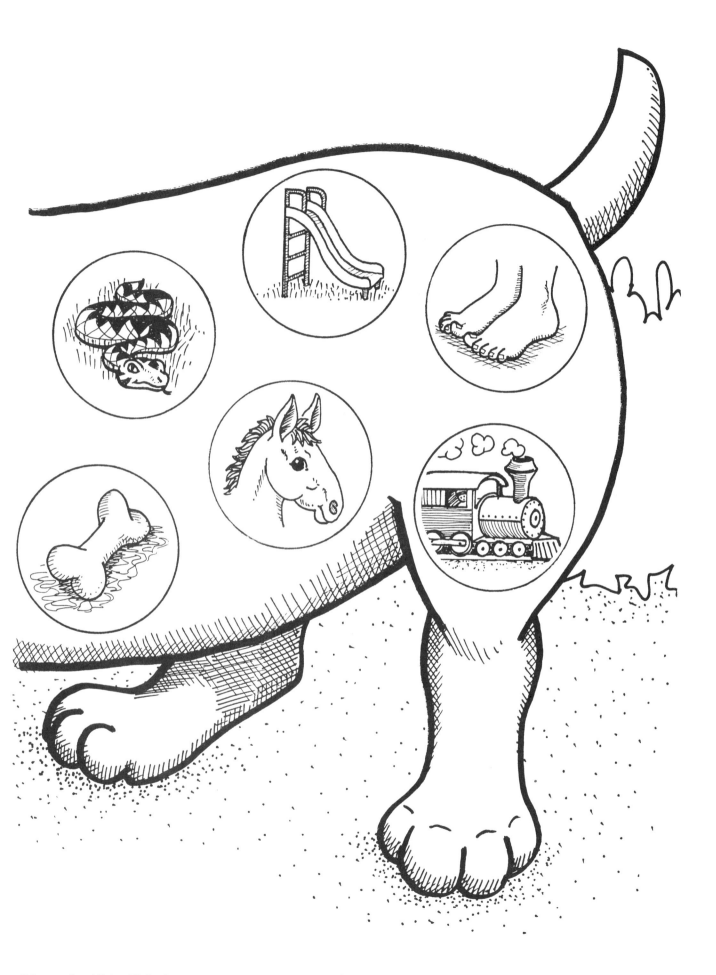

100   IF18974 *Quick Games from Trash*

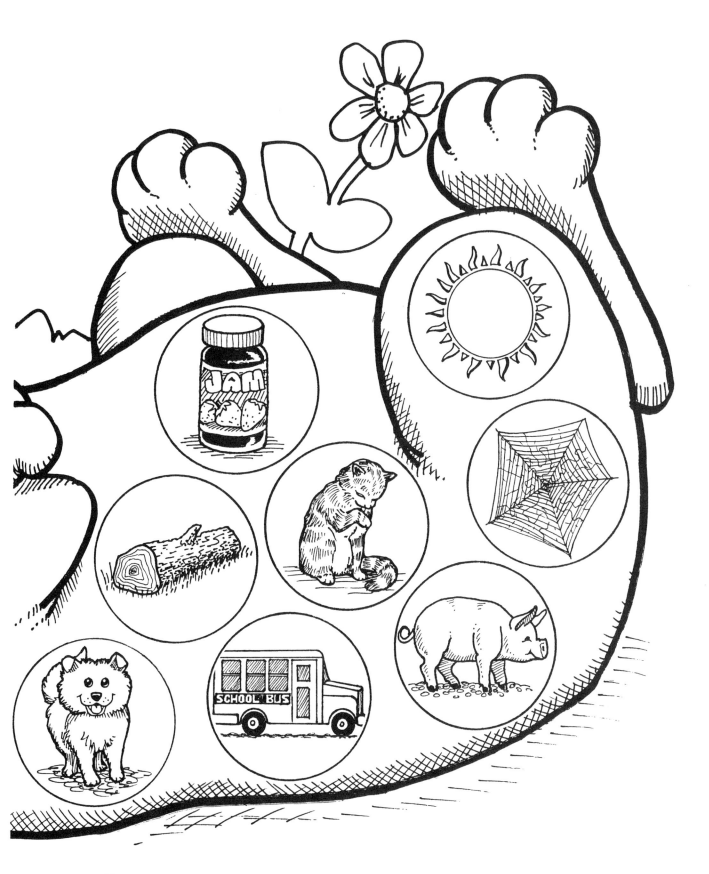

Short Vowel Sounds

 IF18974 *Quick Games from Trash*

Long and Short Vowel Sounds

Dots on Spot Blank Game Board

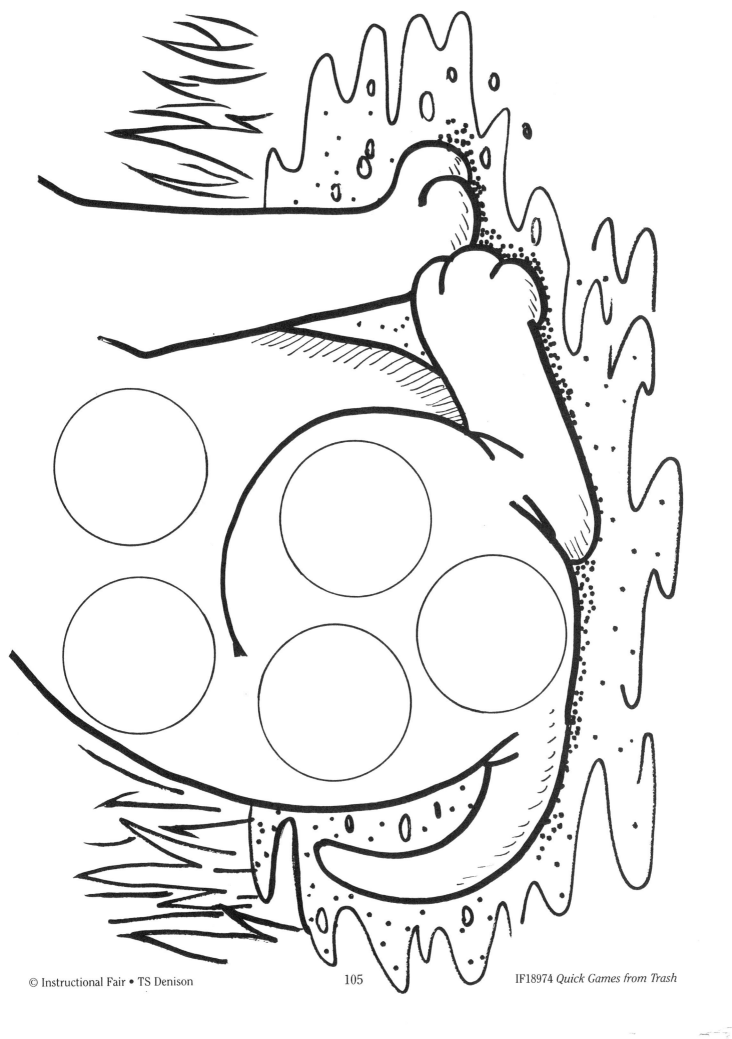

TOSS A WORD

Language Arts

Skill:
Reading words with short vowel sounds

Materials Needed:
- black permanent marker
- handwriting paper (optional)
- one adhesive-backed linoleum tile (at least 10" or 254 mm square)
- pattern page 108
- scissors or utility knife
- shoe box or similar sized box
- twenty empty 35mm film canisters
- white construction paper
- white paper plates, one per player

Directions for Assembly:
1. When purchasing the floor tile square, ask for damaged linoleum tiles. If you mention you are a teacher, the store may reduce the price or donate it to the school. Any design works well; the linoleum is used as a stiff backing for the letter cards.
2. Photocopy the letter card pattern page on white construction paper.
3. Remove the sticky back paper of the linoleum tile.
4. Carefully place the letter card pattern page on the adhesive side of the linoleum tile. Be sure you can read the letters when adhering the pattern page.
5. To finish the letter tiles, cut out each letter square.
6. Place the letter tiles, to make the following short vowel words, inside the film canister. One word should be placed in each film canister. Here are examples of words:

dad	bed	six	mop	sun
can	red	bib	hot	cup
fan	web	wig	box	rug
tag	leg	zip	job	jug

7. Place the film canisters with letter tiles inside a shoe box for storage.
8. On each paper plate draw three connecting squares to create a game board. See illustration.

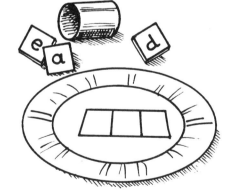

How to Play:

1. Ask two to four children to play the game.
2. Introduce the game to the children by building a word together. Select a canister and paper plate game board. Position the children so that each one can see the game board.
3. Open the canister and drop the letter tiles onto the game board.
4. Ask the children to read the letters.
5. Let the children try to form a word by using only those letters. By trial and error, the children can try different arrangements until they have made the correct word. *Note:* Each of the words have only one vowel which is found in the middle of the word. Discuss how the vowel in the middle of the word has a short sound. Review the short vowel sounds with the children.
6. Give each player a game board and a canister. Have the children follow the same procedure to make the words. Once they have formed their words, they can read them to the teacher. If the words are correct, have the children select different canisters and repeat the procedure.
7. Play continues until the child has made a specified number of words or played for a predetermined length of time.

Other Ideas!

This game certainly works well in a learning center; let the child work independently in creating words with the letter tiles from the canisters. Be sure to include a beginning dictionary for the young learner to use. If several children are interested in forming new words, encourage them to record the words on a chart, adding to the list as new words are discovered.

Toss a Word Pattern

d	a	d	s	i	x
c	a	n	b	i	b
f	a	n	w	i	g
t	a	g	z	i	p
b	e	d	m	o	p
r	e	d	h	o	t
w	e	b	b	o	x
l	e	g	j	o	b
s	u	n	r	u	g
c	u	p	j	u	g

SENTENCE BOARDS

Skill:
Reading simple sentences

Materials Needed:
- assorted vinyl place mats
  (Any design will work but plain place mats work best.)
- cardboard or stiff paper
- green and black permanent markers
- one sheet of construction paper in each color: pink, red, blue, brown, purple, green, white, gray, yellow, and orange
- poster board or stiff paper
- pattern pages 112–124
- scissors
- clear book tape or packing tape
- shoe box or similar sized box
- clear adhesive plastic or laminating material

Directions for Assembly:
1. Cut a rectangle 2" x 7" (51 x 178 mm) from scrap cardboard.
2. Using the rectangle as a pattern tracer, trace one rectangle with the green permanent marker in the top left corner of each vinyl place mat. See the illustration.

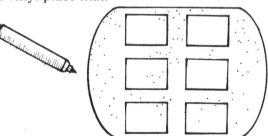

   Note: If the place mat has too many colors or patterns, you can use the back side of the place mat.
3. Using the black permanent marker, trace five more rectangles on the place mat so that there are six total (one in green and five in black) as shown in the illustration.
4. Copy the sentence cards onto the colored construction paper, matching the color listed on the pattern with the construction paper.
5. Cut ten sentence envelopes from poster board or stiff paper. See page 123 for the pattern.
6. Cut out the numeral square from each sentence card pattern and mount them on the envelopes as indicated. See illustration on the next page.

7. Cover the envelope shapes with clear adhesive plastic or laminating material for durability.
8. Finish the envelopes by folding on the dashed lines. Tape where needed.
9. Laminate the 10 colored sheets of construction paper on which the sentence cards have been copied. Cut the sentence cards apart and insert them in the matching sentence envelopes.
10. Store the sentence envelopes inside the cardboard shoe box or a similar sized box.

Sentence Key

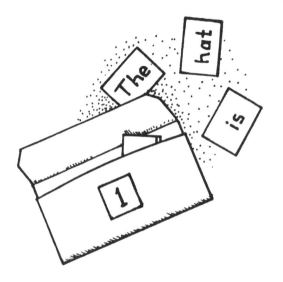

1. (pink) The hat is yellow and red.
2. (red) The spider has five orange spots.
3. (blue) Can you see the big tree?
4. (brown) The girl has a pretty dress.
5. (purple) The boy has a blue shirt.
6. (green) The cat has a toy mouse.
7. (white) Jan will jump over the rock.
8. (gray) Bob will run around the box.
9. (yellow) The goat will eat the coat.
10. (orange) Who is in the red car?

How to Play:

1. Select a small group of children to participate. This activity works best when introduced to a group of four to six children. Once it has been introduced it can be played with a large group of children or used in a learning center.
2. Position the children in a circle around a table or on the floor so they can clearly see the materials. As a cooperative group, complete one sentence board before allowing the children to work independently.
3. Introduce the vinyl place mat board. Show the children that the green rectangle indicates "go" or the first word in the sentence. Discuss how this word must begin with an capital letter since it begins the sentence.
4. Select one sentence envelope to do as an example. Place the cards in random order in clear view of the children. Have the children read each of the words.
5. Ask the children to identify the word that begins the sentence. Place that word in the first green rectangle.

7. Now have the children arrange the remaining words to make a complete sentence. If they are having trouble, they can find the last word in the sentence by locating the word with a punctuation mark. By trial and error, let the children explore different possibilities until they have placed the words in the correct order.
8. Hand out a sentence board for each child in the group.
9. Let each child select a sentence envelope to complete. When the words are placed in the correct order encourage the child to select a different envelope and continue in the same manner.

Other Ideas!

After completing a sentence on their game boards, the children can print the sentences on the recording sheets (see page 124) and then illustrate them.

If you want to ensure that each child completes all of the sentences, a simple recording card can be made. Using a 3" x 5" (76 x 127 mm) index card for each child, place each child's name at the top of a card and write the numbers 1–10. As the child completes a sentence on the recording sheet or on the game board, the number is checked off. This way you can see how many sentences each child has completed and the child also can use the card as a reference.

If some children are ready to read more difficult words, create your own sentence cards (see page 122 for pattern).

(pink)

I

The

hat

is

yellow

and

red.

(red)

2

The

spider

has

five

orange

spots.

(blue)

3

Can

you

see

the

big

tree?

(brown)

4

The

girl

has

a

pretty

dress.

(purple)

5

The

boy

has

a

blue

shirt.

(green)

6

The

cat

has

a

toy

mouse.

(white)

7

Jan

will

jump

over

the

rock.

(gray)

8

Bob

will

run

around

the

box.

(yellow)

9

The
goat
will
eat
the
coat.

(orange)

10

Who

is

in

the

red

car?

Sentence Boards Pattern

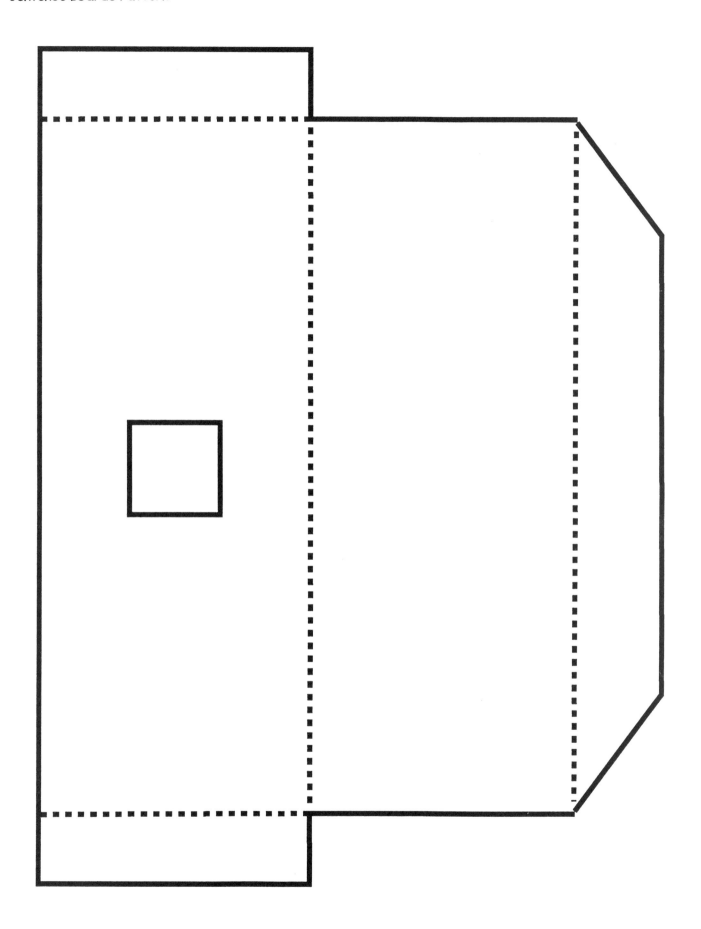

Write a sentence.   Name_____

_____

- -

_____

- -

_____

- -

_____

Draw a picture.

CEREAL BOX PUZZLES

Math

Skill:
Visual discrimination and matching

Materials Needed:
- clear adhesive plastic and laminating material
- construction paper in assorted colors
- four different kinds of children's cereal boxes
- pattern pages 126–129
- permanent markers
- resealable plastic bags and a dress box or pizza box
- scissors and glue

Directions for Assembly:
1. Cut off the front panel of each cereal box to make a puzzle. Trim the panel to 7⅝" x 9½" (194 x 241 mm).
2. Photocopy the patterns on pages 126–129 and mount them on construction paper before laminating them. These will be the base boards for the puzzles.
3. Cover each cereal box panel with clear adhesive plastic.
4. Using the base board patterns, cut each cereal box panel into matching shapes. The puzzle pieces will be placed on the base board.
5. With permanent markers, make a small colored dot on the back of each puzzle piece that matches the color of the base. (For example, mount a base board on red construction paper and then draw a small red dot on the back of each corresponding puzzle piece.) This will color code the puzzle pieces with the base board, making it easier for the children to keep the sets intact.
6. Puzzle pieces can be stored in a plastic bag. Place all the bases and puzzle pieces in a dress box or pizza box.

How to Play:
1. Place the box containing the puzzles in a center.
2. Have the child choose a base board and the corresponding pieces and then assemble the puzzle.

Other Ideas!
To make the activity more difficult, provide puzzle pieces without the base. Color code the puzzle pieces as in the original directions and place them in a resealable plastic bag. Children can assemble the pieces using visual clues.

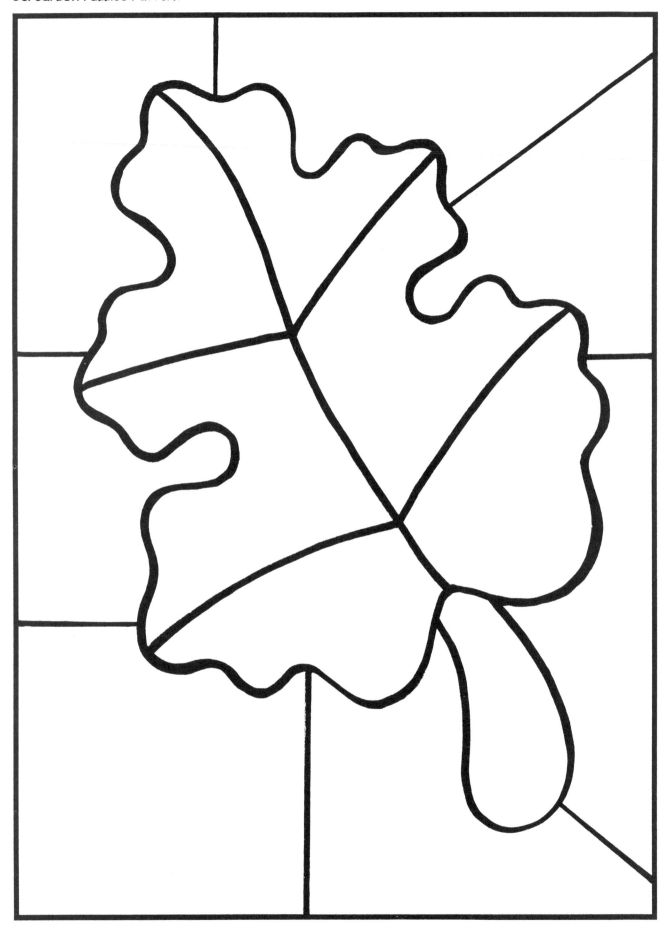

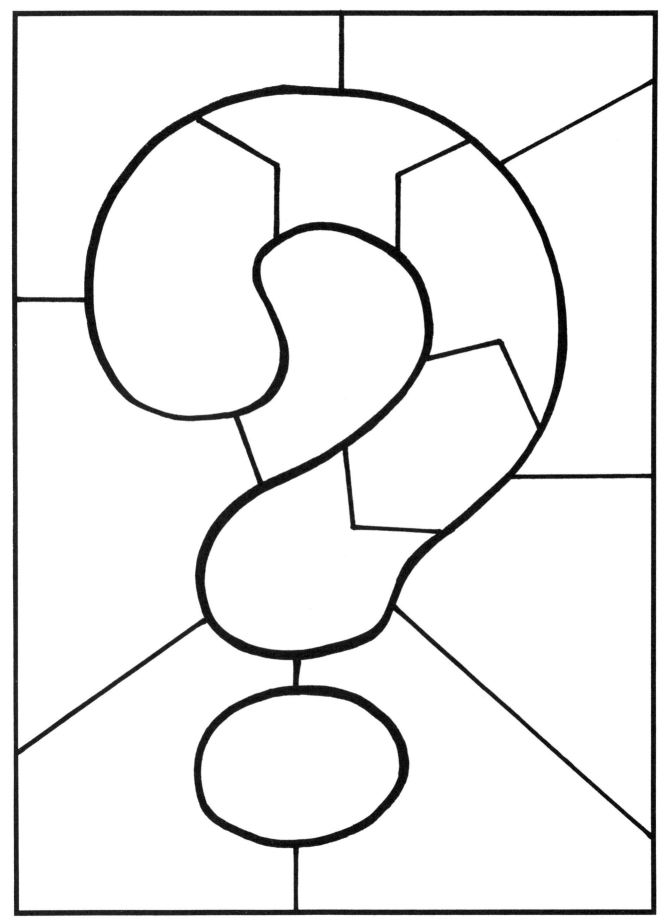

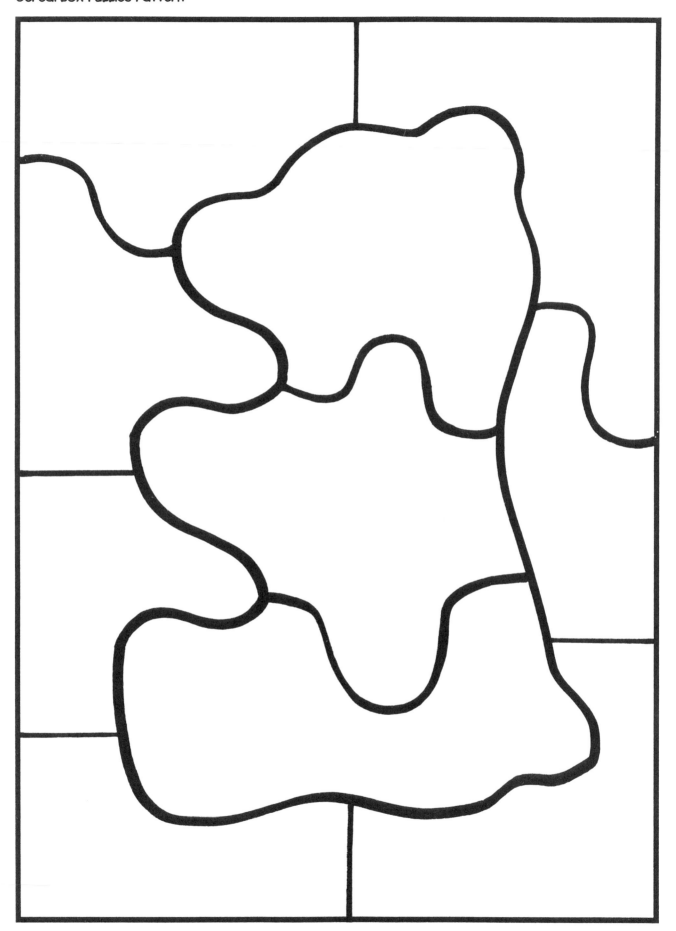

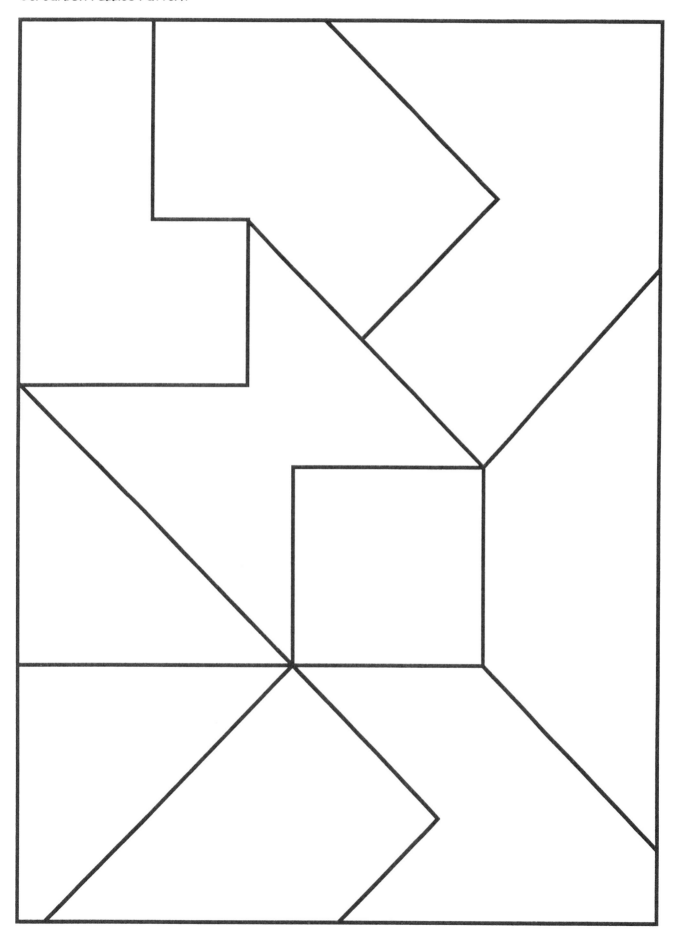

SHADOW SHAPES

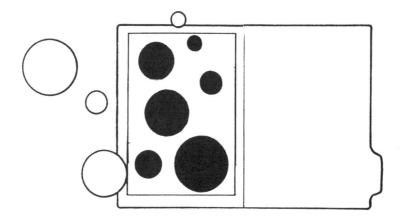

Math

Skill:
Visual discrimination and matching

Materials Needed:
- black construction paper
- clear adhesive plastic or laminating material
- colorful file folders, one for each game board
- glue
- lids from various jars or containers, differing in size
- scissors

Directions for Assembly:
1. Trace each lid on black construction paper and cut out the shapes.
2. Glue the shapes onto the manila folder.
3. Select different sizes of lids and make additional game boards.
4. Laminate the folders or cover them with clear adhesive plastic for durability.

How to Play:
1. Place the lids and the game boards at a small table or learning center location.
2. Invite the children to match the lids with their corresponding "shadows."

Other Ideas:
Looking for more discrimination actitivtes? Search for other junk (or treasures!), items that can become "shadow shapes." Consider small children's toys, math manipulatives, art materials, and so forth. Trace around your new "finds" and set out the materials for more learning fun.

DIGGING FOR TREASURE!

Math

Skill:
Visual discrimination and matching

Materials Needed:
- craft glue
- large plastic tablecloth
- matching pairs of small objects (pennies, buttons, small erasers, shells, beads, rhinestones, etc.)
- permanent marker
- sand or cornmeal
- sand table or large tub
- sand toys such as sifters, shovels, laundry scoops, or spoons
- six small Styrofoam trays

Directions for Assembly:
1. Divide each Styrofoam tray into four sections with the permanent marker.
2. Glue one item of each matching pair to a square on the Styrofoam tray. Each tray will have four items.

How to Play:
1. Fill a sand table or large tub with sand or cornmeal.
2. To make cleanup easier, place the sand table or tub on top of the plastic tablecloth.
3. Hide the remaining items in the sand.
4. Select a small group of children to play, depending on the size of your sand table. One to three players is an ideal group size.
5. Each child selects a tray and take a turn to search for the items shown. Encourage the children to use the sand tools during their searches.
6. Play continues until each child finds the matching items or when the predetermined period of time is finished. *Note:* Children love to play and dig in the sand. You may wish to use a timer to allow each child the same amount of time.

Other Ideas!
If you have more than one matching item of each small object shown on the Styrofoam trays, you may wish to increase the level of difficulty by directing the children to find certain numbers of each object. For example, hide three buttons, four pennies, two red rhinestones, and so on. On the trays print the corresponding number of each kind of item hidden in the sand near the example.

JUNK SORT!

Skill:
Classifying and sorting

Materials Needed:
- cardboard or poster board, 4" x 6" (102 x 152 mm) pieces
- collection of junk or small items (coins, buttons, small shells, small rocks, small shaped erasers, beads, dried seeds, rhinestones, bottle caps, keys)
- craft glue
- permanent markers
- scissors

Directions for Assembly:
1. To prepare the task cards, cut the cardboard or poster board into pieces approximately 4" x 6" (102 x 152 mm). Using a permanent marker, draw a circle on each cardboard piece.
2. Choose four or five examples of the materials that have a common attribute and glue them on a circle. Continue the process until several task cards are prepared. Some suggestions for grouping the sample pieces: junk that is shiny, junk having a point, junk that is round, junk that is smooth, junk with holes, junk that is rough, junk that is a specific color, junk that is not shiny or not round, and so on.
3. Decide how many children will be using the materials simultaneously and then make a blank task card for each player.

How to Play:
1. Select a small group of children to sit around the collection of junk.
2. Each child selects a cardboard task card. Each child must first determine what attribute the items have in common.
3. After the child identifies the attribute, he/she then finds items in the collection that have the same attribute and places them on a blank task card. For example, if the child selected a task card which exhibited items having a circular shape, the child would place additional circular items on the blank task card.
4. When finished have the child select a different task card and repeat the procedure.
5. Before the children begin playing with the materials, decide how long they should work.

Other Ideas!
This activity can easily be made more challenging by creating task cards that indicate two attributes by which to sort. For example, select objects which are shiny and smooth and place them in one pile.

MARVELOUS MUFFIN MATCH

Math

Skill:
Classifying and sorting

Materials Needed:
- 24 paper baking cups
- assorted stickers, two of each design (24 pairs)
- clear adhesive plastic or laminating materials
- light brown or tan construction paper
- pattern page 134
- scissors
- two muffin tins (each holding 12 muffins)

Directions for Assembly:
1. Make four copies of the muffin pattern on tan or light brown construction paper for each muffin tin.
2. Select pairs of stickers to create a matching game.
3. Place one of each pair of stickers on a "muffin."
4. Laminate the "muffins" and then cut them out.
5. Place the other sticker of each pair on the bottom of a paper baking cup.
6. Store the muffin liners in the muffin pans.

How to Play:
1. Place the game in a learning center location.
2. If one child is working with the activity, have the child select a muffin tin and find the matching pairs, placing the corresponding muffin in the correct baking cup.
3. For two children to play, let each child select a muffin tin. Scatter the muffins in random order. Begin play by having the children take turns selecting a muffin and placing it in the corresponding baking cup. Play ends when all matches have been made.

Other Ideas!
A number of variations are possible when preparing the materials for this skill-based game:

Skill	Baking Cup	Muffin
beginning sound	consonant letter	corresponding picture
color words	color sticker	color word
addition	addition fact	sum
counting	numbers	dots to count

Marvelous Muffin Match Pattern

BLUE EYES, BROWN HAIR AND A SMILE

Math

Skill:
Classifying and sorting

Materials Needed:
- construction paper
- glue
- one coffee can
- one small shirt box
- pictures of faces (various ages) from old magazines, catalogs, or colored advertisements
- scissors

Directions for Assembly:
1. To make the picture cards, clip pictures of faces from various sources and glue each one on a square piece of construction paper.
2. Cut a sheet of construction paper to fit the coffee can. Decorate the paper with additional faces. If desired, cover the paper with clear adhesive plastic before gluing it on the can.
3. Store the picture cards in the coffee can.
4. Open the shirt box to create two trays.
5. Write "YES" on one tray and "NO" on the other.

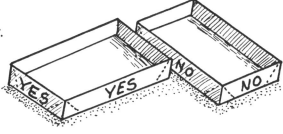

How to Play:
1. Have a small group of children sit in a circle.
2. Begin by discussing their faces and what features their faces have. Some examples: Does anyone have brown hair? Does anyone have freckles?
3. Continue by asking a child to name one feature you just discussed.
4. Have each child select a picture from the can. Encourage them to examine their pictures and then have each one answer the question: Does it have that feature? If it does, place it on the tray marked "YES." If not, place it on the other tray.
5. Repeat the procedure with a different facial feature.

Other Ideas!
Place the picture cards in the middle of a small group of children. Select two facial features and let the children find all picture cards that display those features. Continue sorting in different ways.

MILK CAP PATTERNING

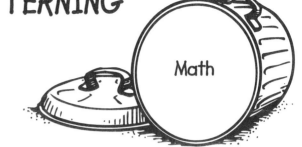

Math

Skill:
Patterning

Materials Needed:
- clear adhesive plastic or laminating material
- glue
- pattern pages 138–139
- 50–60 plastic milk or water jug caps (either snap-on or screw-on lids)
- poster board
- small container with lid
- spray paint in various colors and newspaper (optional)
- watercolored markers (in colors that match the milk caps)
- white construction paper

Directions for Assembly:
1. Build a collection of plastic caps for patterning activities. You will need several of each color collected. *Note:* If you are unable to collect plastic bottle caps in various colors, you can use spray paint to color them. Use several different colors. To do this, lay the caps on newspaper. Spray a thin coat of paint on each one, let it dry, and repeat. When the caps are dry, turn them over and repeat the painting process on the other side. Store the caps in a small container.
2. To make the pattern cards, reproduce several copies of pattern page 138 on white construction paper.
3. Using markers that coordinate with the plastic caps, color the circles with your markers to create patterns that can be matched with the milk caps. Some suggested patterns: ABABAB, ABCABC, ABBABB, AABAAB, AABBAA, ABCCAB, ABACAB, and AABBCC. *Note:* If some children need more sequential practice with patterns, select a simple repeating pattern and create two task cards in different colors.
4. Laminate the pattern cards for duability.

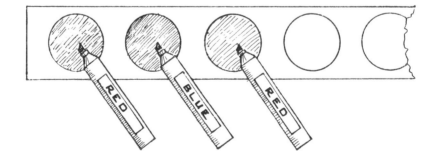

How to Play:

1. Have a small group of children sit near the container of plastic jug caps.
2. Let each child select a pattern strip.
3. To begin play, encourage the child to place corresponding plastic caps on the circles and then continue the pattern. The play ends when all milk caps are used or the pattern repeats the number of times designated by the teacher.
4. Encourage the children to continue making patterns by selecting new task cards.
5. Play continues for a specified time or until a certain number of patterns have been completed.
6. If you wish to have the children record their patterns, provide copies of the recording sheet (see page 139) and corresponding crayons.

Other Ideas!

For a three-dimensional patterning activity that is more challenging to complete, collect a variety of caps in various sizes and colors and create patterns with them on heavy cardboard. Be sure to supply extra caps for children to use. To play, have each child select a pattern card as in the original game and continue the patterns using colors and shapes of caps.

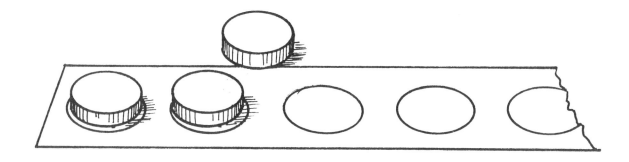

Milk Cap Patterning Strips

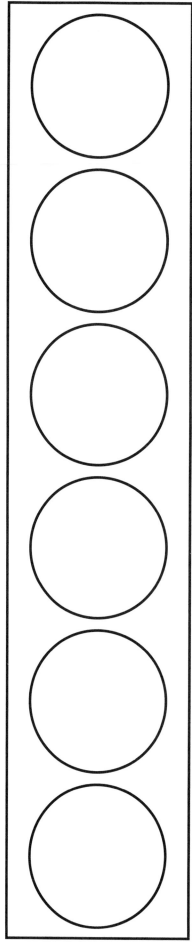
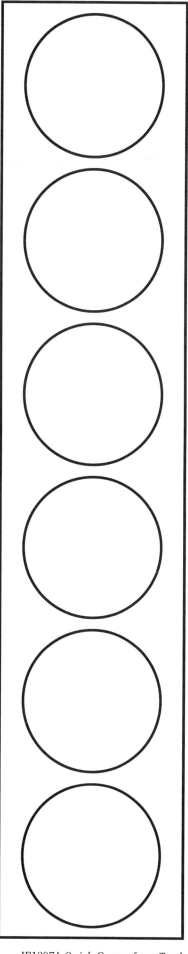

Milk Cap
Patterning Strips

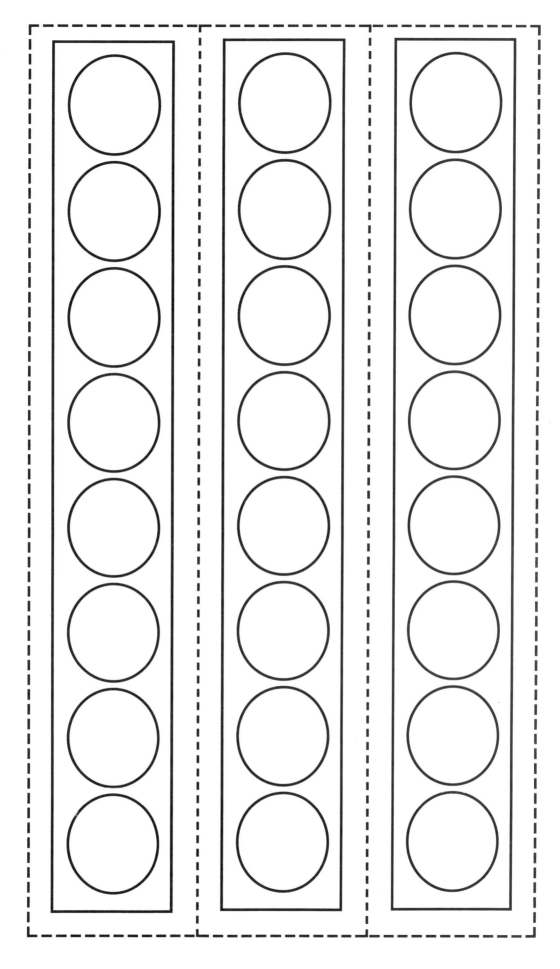

PUSH-UP PATTERNING

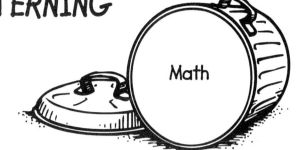

Skill:
Patterning

Materials Needed:
- clear adhesive plastic or laminating material
- paper towels
- pattern page 141
- permanent marker
- set of children's stamps, any designs (inexpensive rubber stamps attached to small foam squares)
- several plastic inserts from push-up ice cream treats
- scissors and tacky glue
- Styrofoam tray
- tempera paint, two different colors
- white construction paper

Directions for Assembly:
1. Using glue, mount a stamp on the end of each push-up ice cream stick, then set aside to dry.
2. With the permanent marker, draw a small dot on the top surface of the push-up stick to indicate the top of the stamp. This will help the children stamp the pictures correctly on their papers.
3. To make a stamp pad, lay a few layers of paper toweling on the Styrofoam tray and moisten them with the liquid paint. Be sure to make the paper moist, not saturated, with paint. If you want to provide stamp pads in different colors, repeat the process for each color of liquid paint.
4. Copy several pattern strips (see page 141) onto white construction paper.
5. Using the push-up stamps, create various patterns that the children can duplicate and continue. Some examples: ABABAB, AABBAA, ABBABB, ABCABC, ABACAB, ABCDAB, and AABBCC.
6. Cover the pattern strips with clear adhesive plastic or laminate them.
7. Reproduce several blank pattern strips and cut them apart.

How to Play:
1. Have each child select a pattern strip.
2. Let the child study the pattern and then use the stamps to duplicate it on the blank pattern strips.
3. Encourage the child to complete several patterns.
4. If interested, allow the children to create their own patterns on the blank pattern strips.

Other Ideas!
Many activities can be completed with stamps. Be creative! Perhaps your young learners need additional experiences with counting or one-to-one correspondence.

Push-Up Patterning Pattern

BARRETTES AND BRAIDS

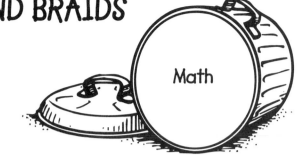

Math

Skill:
Patterning

Materials Needed:
- clear adhesive plastic or laminating material
- collection of children's barrettes (collected from garage sales, donated by parents, or purchased at discount stores)
- construction paper (various skin colors)
- container
- craft knife
- masking tape
- pattern pages 144–145
- scissors
- stiff paper or poster board, 9" x 12" (229 x 305 mm) in size
- twelve 10" (254 mm) lengths of yarn (represent hair—yellow, brown or black)
- two small rubber bands, one set per activity card
- watercolor markers, colored pencils, or pastels

Directions for Assembly:
1. Choose a face pattern and photocopy it on an appropriate color of construction paper.
2. Using art materials, color the facial features and hair.
3. Cut out the face and mount it on stiff paper or poster board.
4. Cover it with clear adhesive plastic or laminate it.
5. Using the craft knife, make a small slit on either side of the face, just under the bow.
6. Hold six strands of yarn together and push them through the slit, pushing through about ½" (13 mm) of the yarn. Secure the ends on the back side of the picture with a piece of masking tape. Repeat the procedure on the other side of the face.
7. To form the braids, separate the strands into three groups of two strands each. Braid the yarn and secure the end with a rubber band. Repeat the same procedure with the other side. When finished, you will have two braids, one on each side of the face.

8. Using your assortment of barrettes, create a pattern down the left braid. You can create a pattern with colors, shapes, or sizes of the barrettes. Be sure to provide several sets of identical barrettes for the children to use.
9. Place the remaining barrettes in a container.

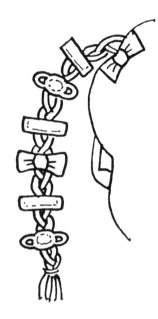

How to Play:
1. Invite a child to work on the activity.
2. The child identifies the pattern you have created with the barrettes.
3. Using the remaining barrettes, let the child make the same pattern on the other braid. The purpose of the activity is to not copy the barrettes used but use the barrettes to show another possibility for a color pattern or shape pattern.
4. Play can continue with another child working to follow the pattern or the teacher can create a new pattern for the child to follow.

Other Ideas!
Collect children's barrettes that have flat surfaces on which you can write with a permanent marker. One suggestion is to number the barrettes and have the children arrange them in numerical order.

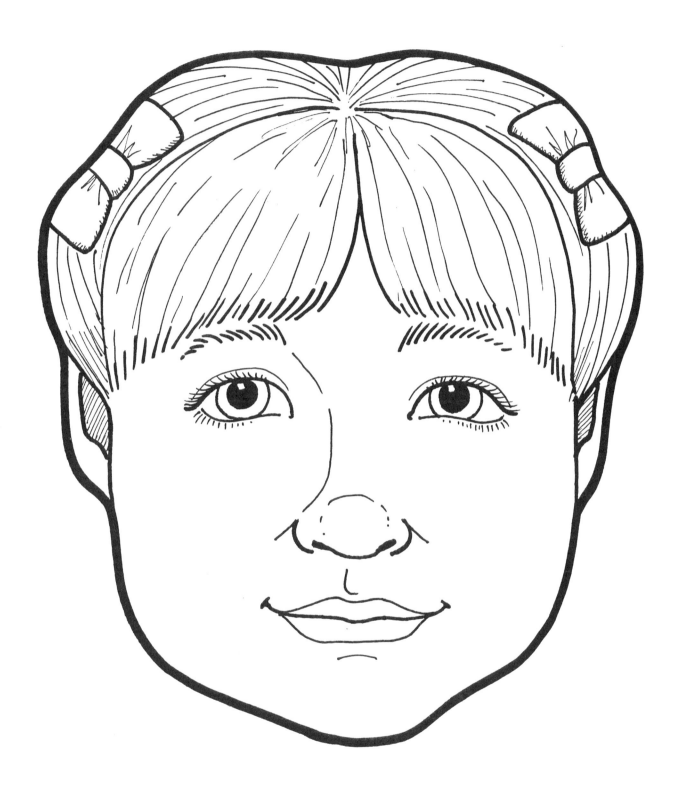

COUNTING BOXES

Math

Skill:
Counting 1–10

Materials Needed:
- construction paper
- contact paper
- facial tissue or baby wipes
- grease pencil
- laminating material or clear adhesive plastic
- one shoe box, shirt box or any other box with a lid
- pattern pages 148–154
- various small inexpensive toys and common items (small plastic people, cowboys, buttons, small erasers, small shells) or any math manipulatives

Directions for Assembly:
1. Cover the box and lid with contact paper.
2. Photocopy the task cards and mount them on construction paper.
3. Laminate the task cards for durability.
4. Place the objects to be counted, the task cards, a grease pencil, and facial tissue in the box.

To Play the Game:
1. Place the box in the math learning center and make it available for independent work.
2. To use the materials, have the child remove only the task cards, grease pencil, and tissue from the box, leaving the small counting objects inside.

3. Let the child select a task card and place an object from the box on each "X," counting each object as she places it.
4. With the grease pencil, the child writes the correct number in the box on the task card.
5. Play continues for a specified time or until all of the task cards have been completed.

Other Ideas!

Additional practice on other math skills can be provided with task cards and manipulatives. If the children are ready to count to 25 have them use a different counting card (see page 154). For addition tasks cards, duplicate several copies of the blank task card pattern on page 153 and then write your own problems. See illustration. Have the child place the small counting objects on the "X" and then write the sum of the two boxes in the square. Perhaps the child is working on simple multiplication facts. Create appropriate problems to reinforce those concepts.

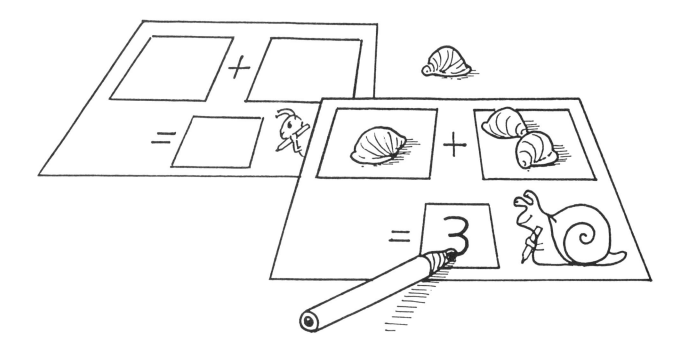

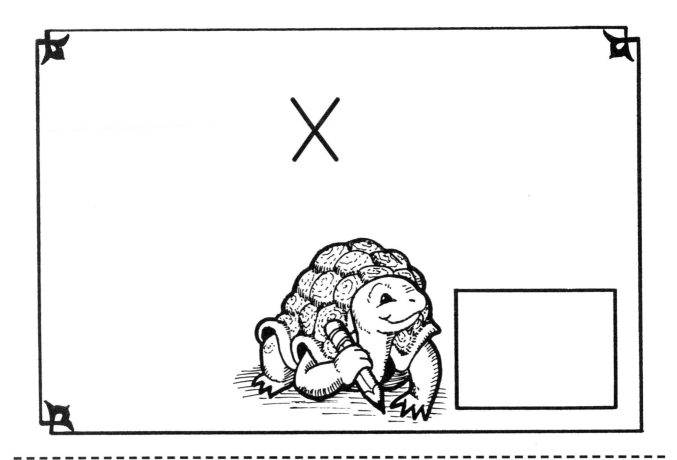

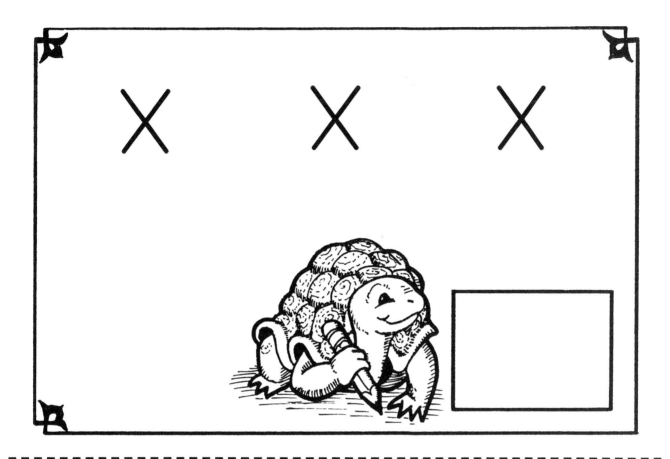

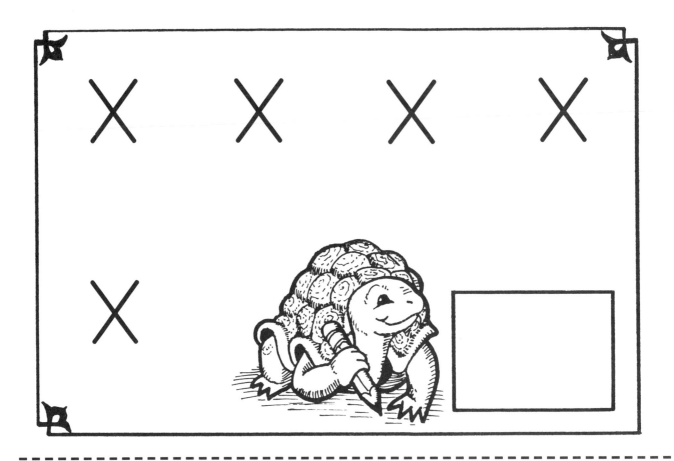

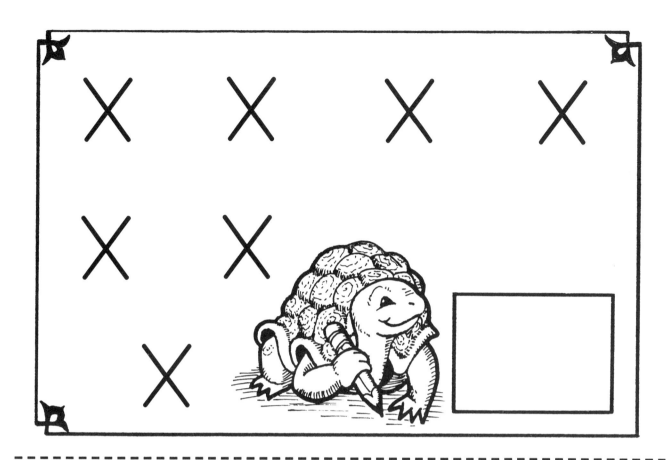

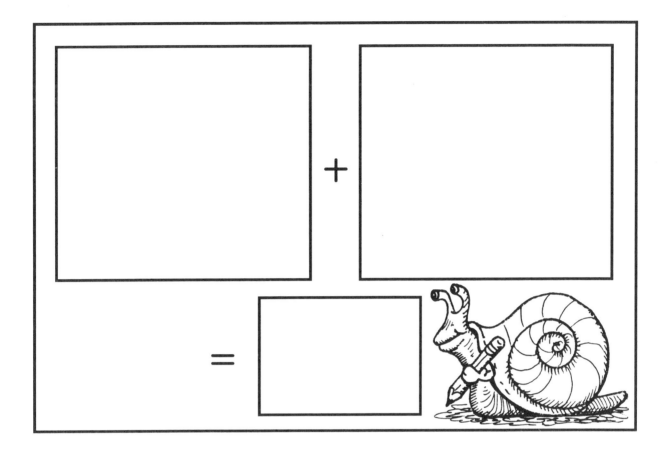

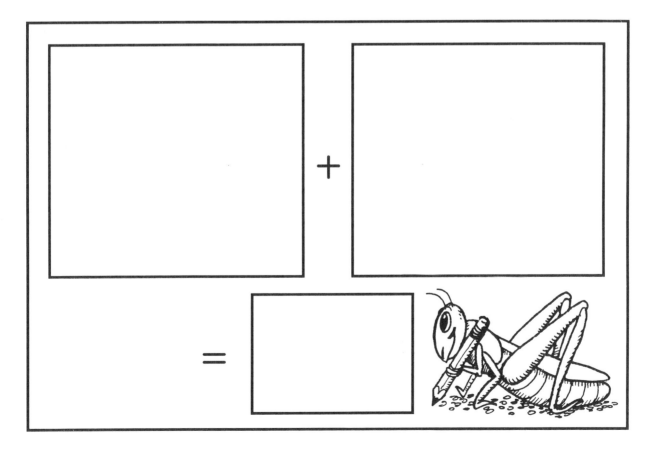

CURLY CATERPILLAR

Skill:
Counting from 1–10

Math

Materials Needed:
- clear adhesive plastic or laminating materials
- colored construction paper to match plastic lids
- 35 screw-on or snap-on lids from milk or water jugs (same color lids)
- pattern pages 156–159
- permanent markers
- resealable plastic bag

Directions for Assembly:
1. Select the pattern for Curly Caterpillar that you choose to use. Pattern #1 shows sets of dots in numerical order. Pattern #2 (page 157) and Pattern #3 (pages 158-159) are blank for designing games that feature higher numbers or sets shown in random order.
2. Photocopy the selected game pattern on colored construction paper.
3. If needed, draw sets of dots for the children to count.
4. Laminate the pattern page or cover it with clear adhesive plastic.
5. Using a permanent marker, write numbers 1–10 or other corresponding numerals on each set of plastic lids.
6. Store the plastic caps in a plastic resealable bag.

How to Play:
The child removes the lids from the plastic bag and places them on the corresponding circles on the caterpillar.

Other Ideas!
Use the blank pattern on page 157 or pages 158-159 to create game boards that reinforce other skills: for example, match capitals to lowercase letters, addition equations to sums, colors to color words, beginning consonant sound pictures to letters, identical stickers, shapes, and so on.

Curly Caterpillar Pattern

STICKER STRIPS

Math

Skill:
Number recognition 1–10 or 11–20

Materials Needed:
- can with lid
- clear adhesive plastic or laminating material
- colored construction paper
- glue or tape
- pattern pages 162–163
- scissors
- ten different animal stickers (or stamps), five of each kind
- three or four sheets of white construction paper
- watercolor markers (optional)

Directions for Assembly:
1. Photocopy the pattern for the sticker strip from page 162 or 163 on white construction paper.
2. Place a sticker, stamp, or draw a colored circle above each number. Make sure that each sticker, stamp, or circle is different and that the children can identify them. Choose animals that the children can name. For example, do not use stickers that show different breeds of dogs. The dogs will all look different; it will be hard to describe where you want the child to look on the sticker sheet if he or she cannot name each breed of dog.

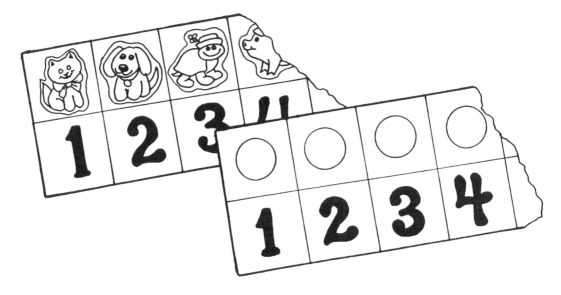

3. Cut out the sticker strips sections and glue or tape them together to make one strip.
4. In order for a small group of children to play with the materials, make three more identical sticker strips.
5. Cover the finished strips with clear adhesive plastic or laminate them.
6. Cover the can with construction paper and decorate as desired.
7. To prepare the game cards, cut ten small squares from colored construction paper.
8. On each game card place a matching sticker that corresponds with the sticker strip.
9. Laminate the game cards. Cut them apart and store them in the container.

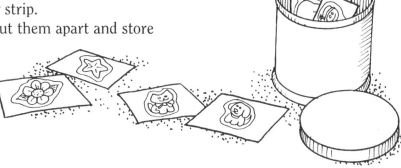

How to Play:

1. Select three or four children for the game and give each child a sticker strip.
2. The first child reaches into the can and draws a game card. The child names the picture.
3. Each player locates that picture on a sticker strip and tries to name the number written underneath.
4. The game card is returned to the can and the next child draws out a game card.
5. The game continues until every child has had the opportunity to name several numbers.

Other Ideas!

This activity can easily be played like a game. Place a small container of corn, pennies, erasers, or any small manipulative within reach of the children playing. The game is played in the same manner, except that the child who draws the card is given the opportunity to name the number first. If the child is correct, she takes a small item from the container. If the child is incorrect, another child is given the opportunity to correctly name the number and earn an item from the container. Play continues until each child has had several tries or has played the game for a predetermined length of time. The child with the most items collected is declared the winner.

Sticker Strips Pattern

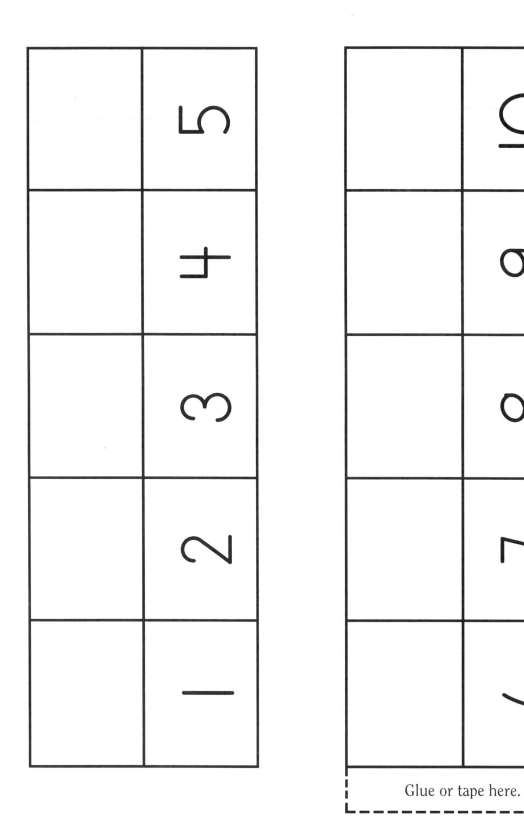

Glue or tape here.

	15	14	13	12	11

	20	19	18	17	16

Glue or tape here.

WHICH WHEELS?

Math

Skill:
Numerical order (1–1000)

Materials Needed:
- 10–20 identical snap-on plastic lids from milk or water jugs, two lids for each car made
- clear adhesive plastic or laminating material
- construction paper, one sheet for each car
- clean plastic container with lid
- pattern pages 165–167
- permanent markers
- scissors

Directions for Assembly:
1. Photocopy page 165 to make three or four task cards.
2. On each car write a number in the center.
3. Laminate the task cards or cover them with clear adhesive plastic for durability.
4. Select two lids as the wheels for each car. Write the number that comes before the number on the car for the left wheel. Write the number that comes after the number on the car for the right wheel.
5. Store the wheels in a container that has a lid.

How to Play:
1. Encourage a small group of children to play the game. Let each child select a task card.
2. All of the wheels are placed in a container from which the children can draw but are unable to see the wheels.
3. Play begins with the first child reaching into the can and selecting a wheel. If number on the wheel completes the numerical order, the wheel is placed on the car. If the wheel does not match, it is returned to the can.
4. The next player takes a turn by drawing a wheel from the can.
5. Play continues until one child completes a car or until all children have collected their wheels.

Other Ideas!
Use pattern pages 166-167 as an independent activity. Write numbers on the vehicles and lids in the same manner. Have the child place the wheels on the corresponding cars.

165

Which Wheels? Game Board

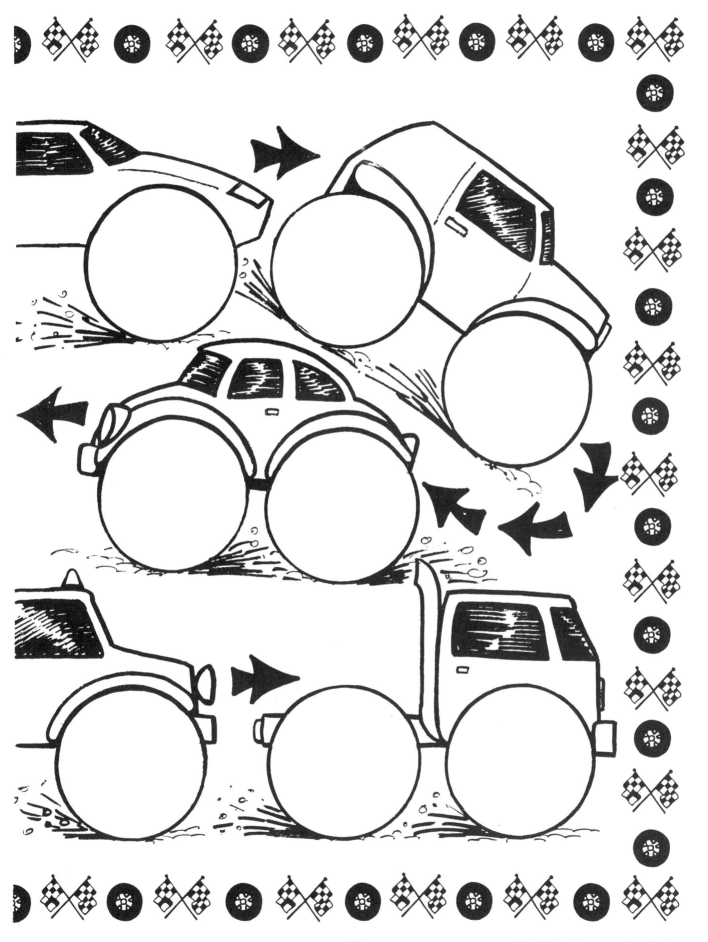

MILK CAP SEQUENCE

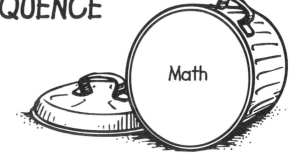

Math

Skill:
Numerical order with numbers 1–10 or 10–100

Materials Needed:
- 24 caps from plastic milk containers or water jugs,
  eight lids in three different colors (either screw-on or snap-on lids)
- clear adhesive plastic or laminating material
- glue
- pattern pages 169–175
- permanent markers
- scissors
- three colorful file folders
- three resealable plastic bags

Directions for Assembly:
1. Copy the patterns on pages 170–175.
2. Mount matching game board patterns on file folders. If you are able to use three colors of lids for your game pieces, then draw a matching colored dot on the corresponding file folder game to let the child know which pieces are used with each game board.
3. Cover the game boards with clear adhesive plastic or laminate for durability.
4. For Game A, use a permanent marker to write the numbers 8, 4, 3, 10, 5, 9, 6, and 7 on eight identical plastic lids of one color.
5. For Game B, use a permanent marker to write the numbers 8, 3, 6, 5, 4, 9, 2, and 7 on eight identical lids of one color.
6. For Game C, use a permanent marker to write the numbers 6, 2, 5, 4, 7, 3, 1, and 8 on eight identical lids of one color.
7. Store the game pieces in plastic bags.

How to Play:
1. Have the child select a game board and the corresponding game pieces.
2. To play, encourage the child to place the game pieces on the corresponding spaces to arrange the numbers in numerical order.

Other Ideas!
Use the blank game board pattern on page 169 to create new games using larger numbers to sequence. You may wish to change the numbers on pattern pages 170–175 for additional games.

Milk Cap Sequence Blank Pattern

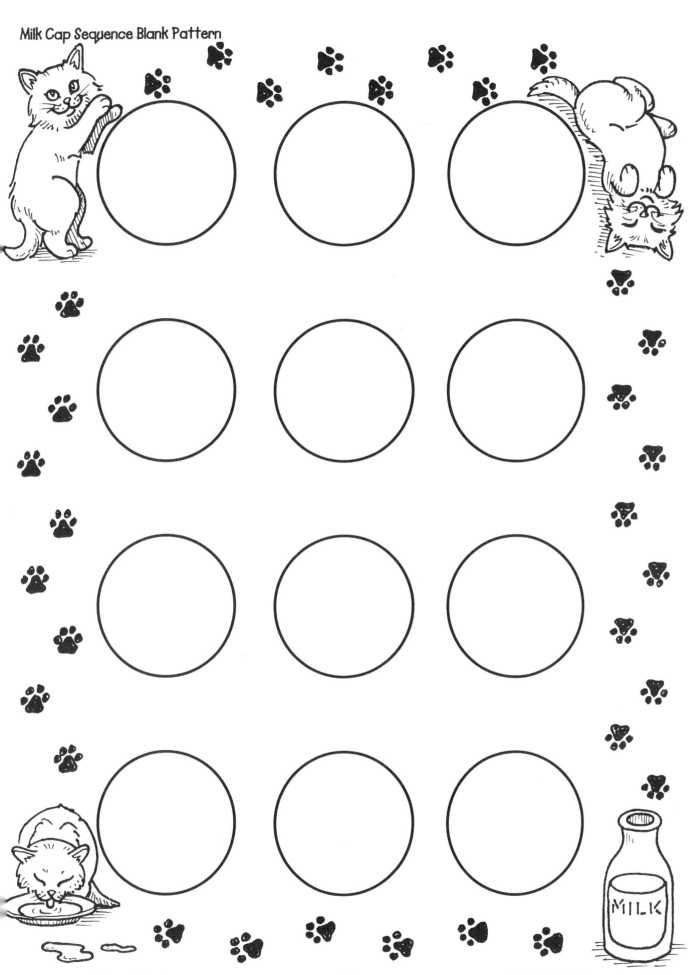

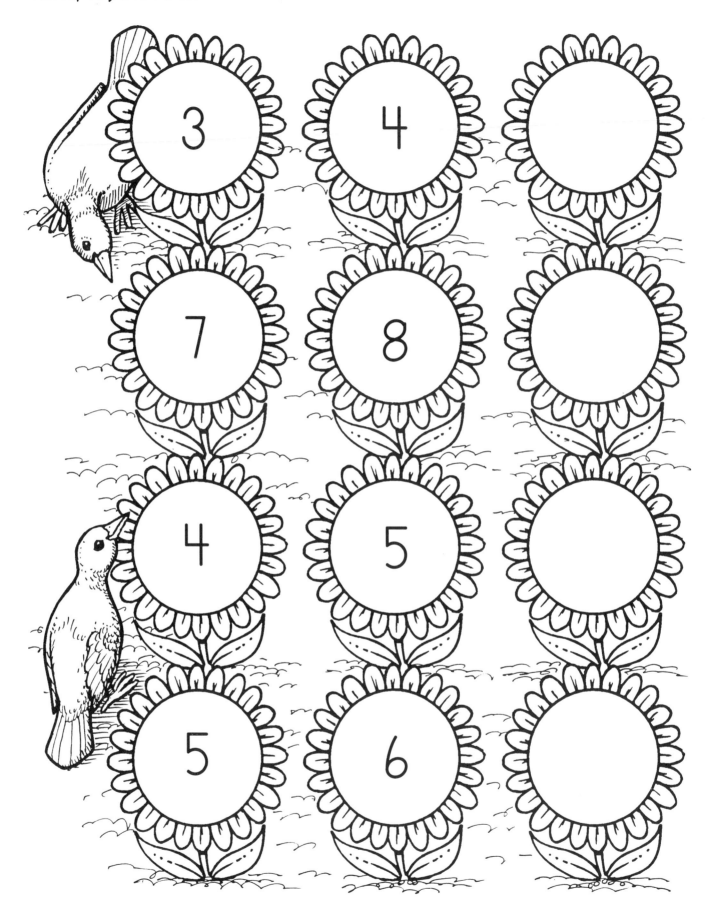

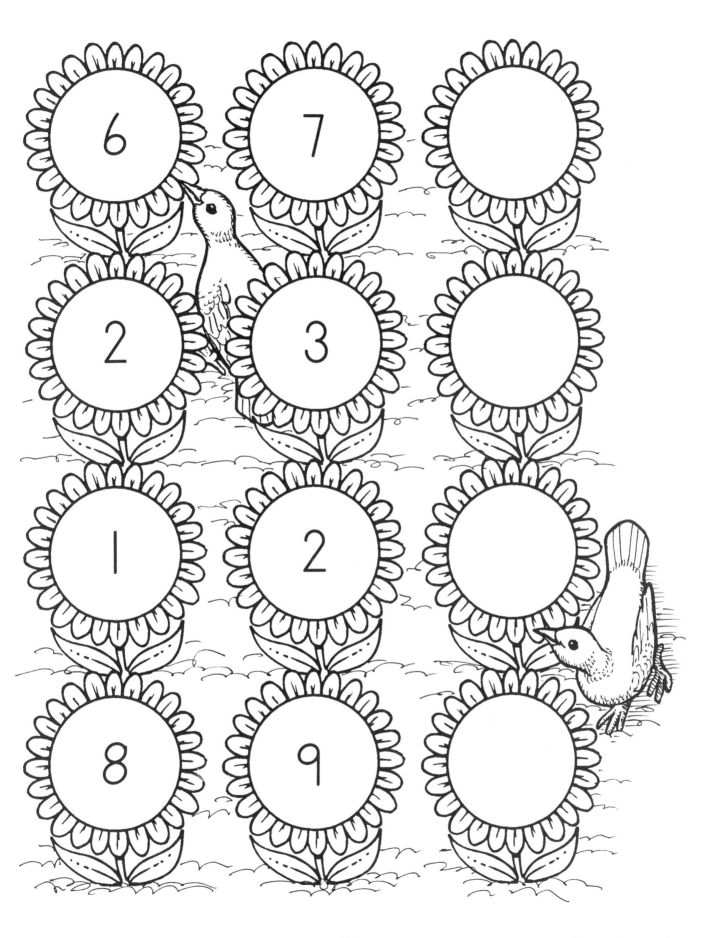

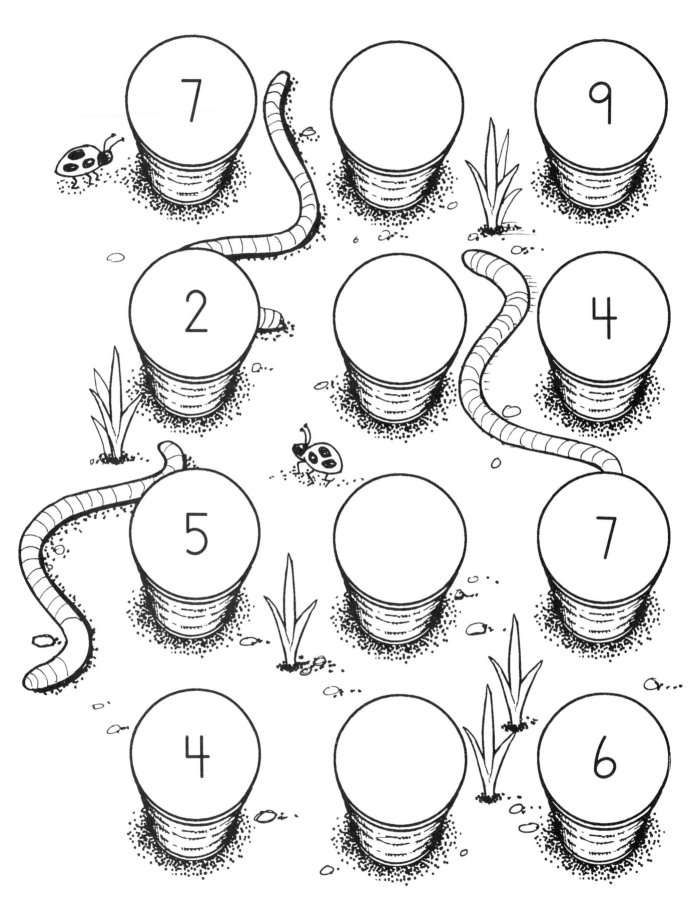

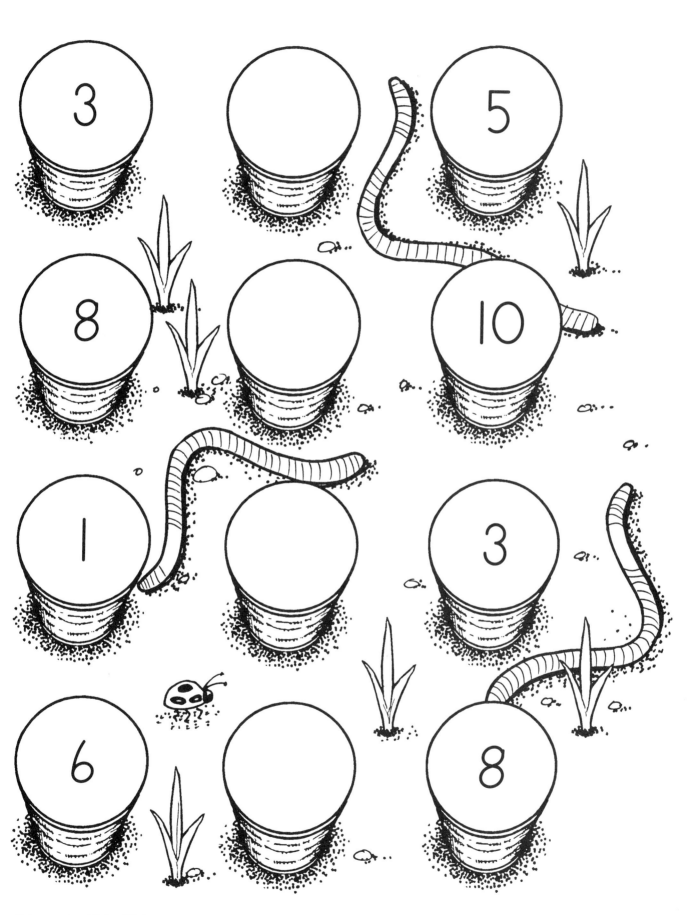

STICKS IN ORDER

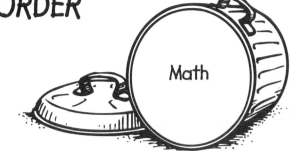

Skill:
Numerical order 1–49, 50–99, or 100–149

Materials Needed:
- 50 craft sticks
- five large plastic lids from liquid laundry detergent bottles
- permanent markers (red, yellow, green, orange, and blue)

Directions for Assembly:

1. Using a permanent marker, write the following numbers, one set on each lid. The lids will be used as cups to hold the craft sticks, so the original top of the lid will now be the "base." Choose the series of numbers that are appropriate for your students and then write the numbers on the bases:
   - 1–9, 10–19, 20–29, 30–39, 40–49;
   - 50–59, 60–69, 70–79, 80–89, 90–99; or
   - 100–109, 110–119, 120–129, 130–139, 140–149.

2. With the permanent marker, number the crafts sticks from 1–49 (or 50–99 or 100–149).

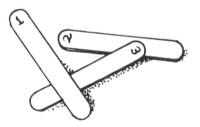

3. Place a green line under 1, 10, 20, 30, and 40 (or 50, 60, 70, 80, and 90, or 100, 110, 120, 130, and 140). This designates the beginning number in each cup.

4. To label the sticks and cups use a colored dot system. For example, on the backs of the sticks 1–9 draw a small red dot. Place a small red dot on the base of the cup marked 1–9. At a quick glance the children can see that the sticks with the red dots belong in the cup with the red dot.
5. Continue coding the other sticks and cups with corresponding dots: blue, green, yellow, and orange. Each cup's color and number should match the ones on the sticks.
6. Place the sticks in the appropriate cups with the numbers showing.

How to Play:

1. Invite five children to play the game. Give each a game cup.
2. Have the children remove the sticks from their game cups.
3. Each child determines the first number by looking for the green line and then arranges the sticks in numerical order.
4. Play can continue by having the children trade game cups and then arrange those sticks in order.

Other Ideas!

The level of difficulty can be changed by sequencing sets of numbers that do not begin with 10s. For instance, the sticks can be labeled with numbers 13–23, 36–46, and so on. You can also make additional games for numbers larger than 150.

THE GREAT HAMBURGER RACE

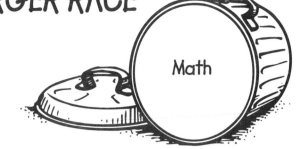

Math

Skill:

Numerical order 100–200
(identifying the number that is one more)

Materials Needed:

- clear adhesive plastic or laminating material
- pattern pages 179–185
- watercolor markers
- scissors
- six fast food carry out bags (contact a local fast food restaurant for donations)
- six sheets of white construction paper
- six small paper plates
- small resealable plastic bag
- light tan or brown construction paper

Directions for Assembly:

1. Duplicate six copies of pattern page 179 on white construction paper and color them with markers.
2. Store a set of sandwich ingredients in each fast food bag along with a paper plate.
3. Photocopy the hamburger game cards on light tan or brown construction paper.
4. Laminate or cover all of the game pieces with clear adhesive plastic and then cut them apart.
5. Store the game cards in a small plastic bag.

How to Play:

1. Let two to six children play the game, giving each player a fast food bag of game pieces.
2. Each child removes the paper plate from a bag and places it on the table.
3. Set the game cards *face down* in the center of the group of children.
4. The first child draws a game card and identifies the number which is *one more* than shown.
5. If the child is correct, she removes one ingredient for the hamburger from the bag and places it on the paper plate.
6. If the child is incorrect, nothing is removed from the bag and the next child draws a card.
7. Play continues until a child draws a sad face hamburger game card. That player must return one sandwich ingredient to the bag. If the child did not have any ingredients on her plate, play just continues to the next child.
8. The game ends when the first child completes a sandwich by earning all of the ingredients.

Other Ideas!

For other variations, use the blank game card pattern on page 185 to provide different game cards. Some additional skill ideas: beginning sounds, sight words, math facts, and so on.

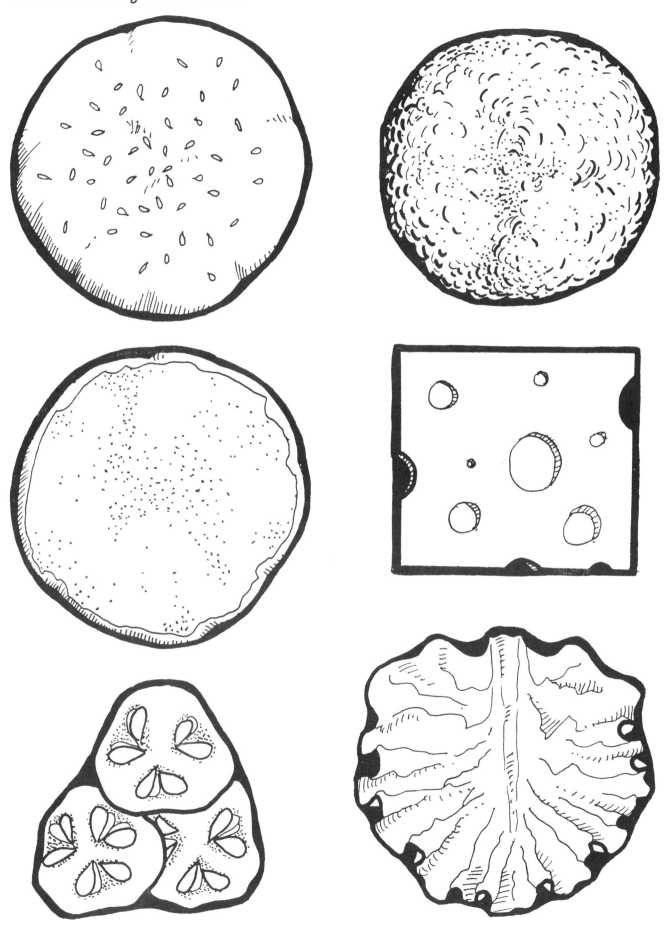

119 _____

125 _____

131 _____

147 _____

159 _____

166 _____

180 _____

121 _____

179 _____

139 _____

192 _____

199 _____

The Great Hamburger Race Patterns

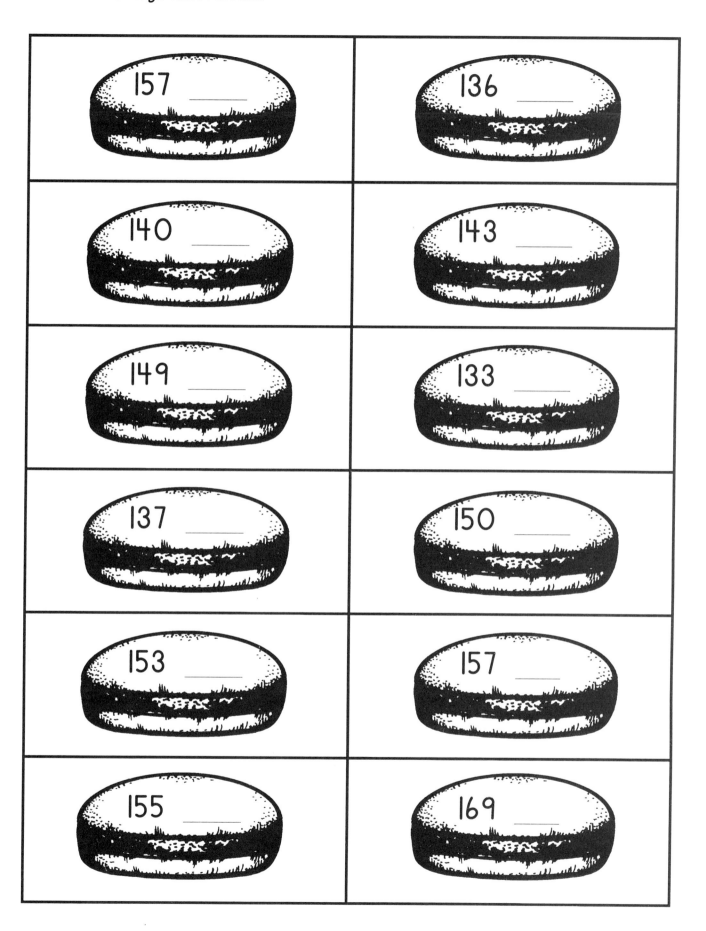

The Great Hamburger Race Patterns

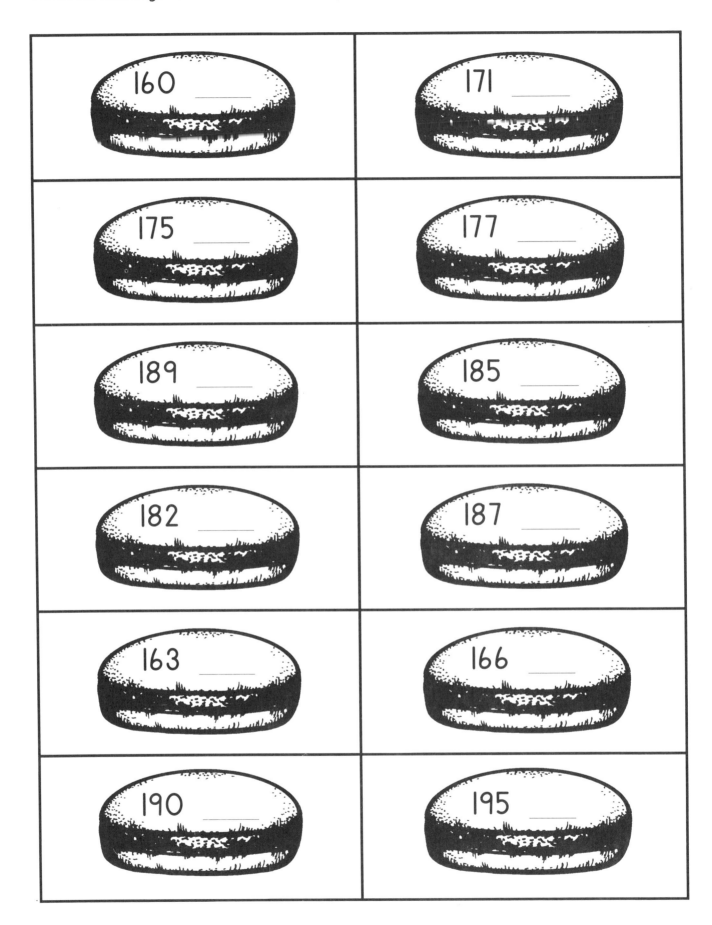

The Great Hamburger Race Patterns

The Great Hamburger Race Patterns

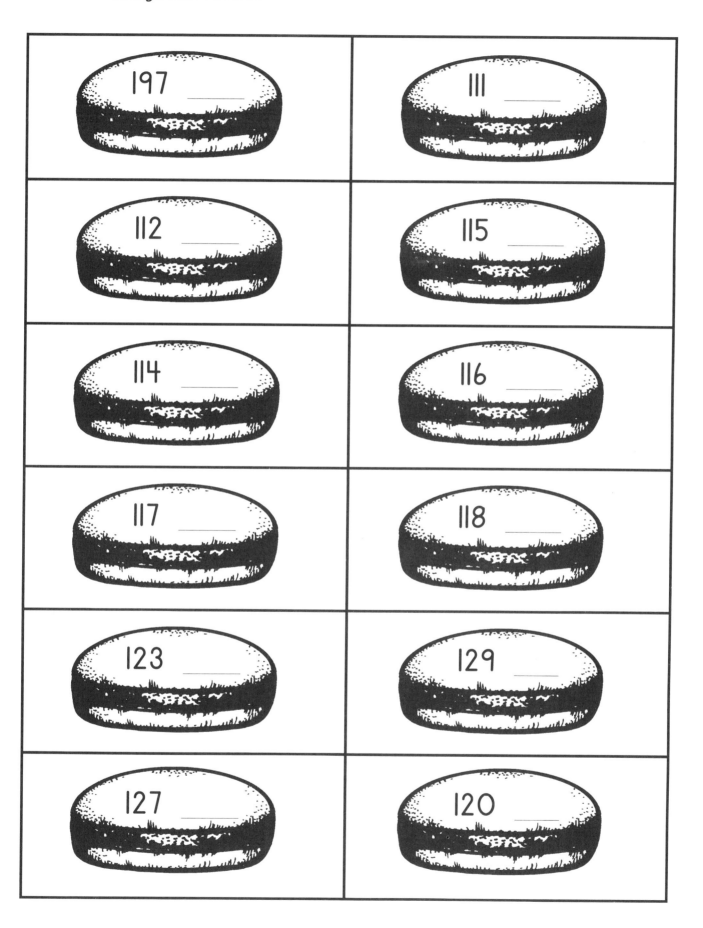

197 _____   111 _____

112 _____   115 _____

114 _____   116 _____

117 _____   118 _____

123 _____   129 _____

127 _____   120 _____

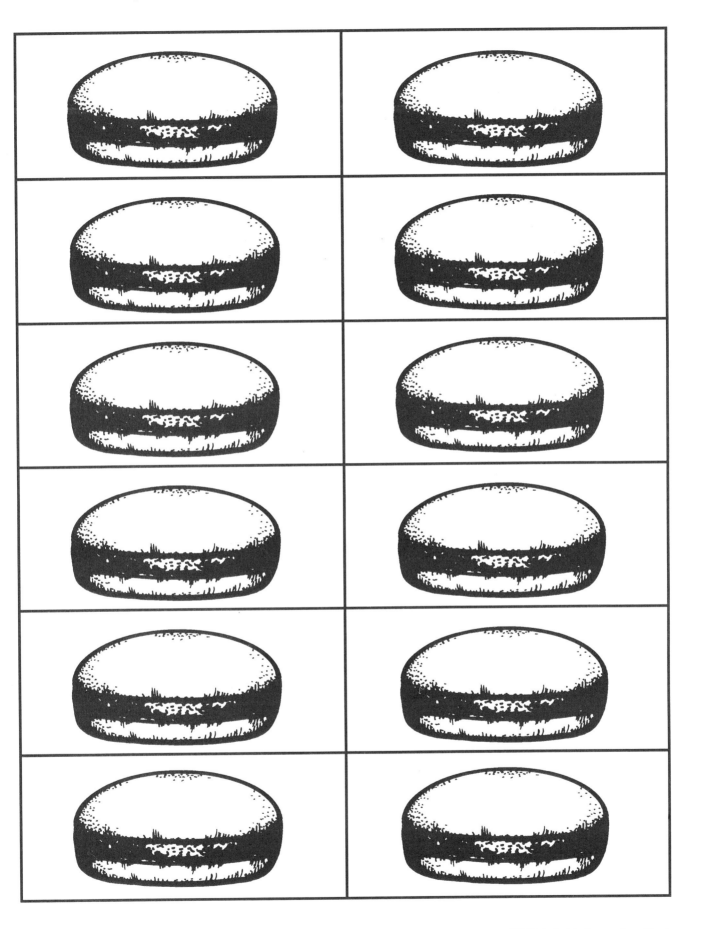

MARBLE MAZE

Skill:
Counting by 10s

Materials Needed:
- clear adhesive plastic or laminating material
- craft glue
- one marble
- one piece of 8" x 12" (203 x 305 mm) craft foam
- one plastic lid from a large container of ice cream or frozen yogurt
- one sheet of construction paper
- pattern pages 188–189
- craft knife or sharp scissors

Directions for Assembly:
1. Copy the pattern on page 188 onto the construction paper. (Enlarge it to fit on the plastic lid.)
2. Cut out the circle and cover it with clear adhesive plastic.
3. Place the circle inside the plastic lid, using craft glue to keep it in place. *Note:* The lip of the plastic lid will keep the marble from rolling off the game board.
4. Using the pattern on page 189, cut the craft foam into a circle and then cut out the small circles by using a sharp pair of scissors or a craft knife.
5. Glue the foam circle on top of the construction paper circle, inside the plastic lid. Make sure the circles match up before mounting the foam circle.
6. Allow the game to dry before adding the marble.

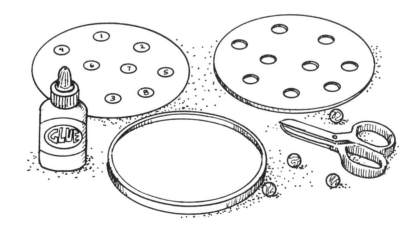

How to Play:

1. Choose two or three children to play the game.
2. To begin play, have the first player place the marble in the number 10 hole.
3. The player must gently tilt the game board to allow the marble to roll but not leave it.
4. The player attempts to roll the marble into each hole, in order, from 10 to 100.
5. If the player rolls it into another hole by mistake, the game board is passed to the next child.
6. Play continues until each child has had a try or until one of the players successfully rolls the marble correctly. A time limit can also be placed to allow for several tries by each player.

Other Ideas!

An easy version of the game can be made by using a cookie sheet (or round cake pan) and a Ping-Pong ball. Use a larger piece of craft foam and cut the holes large enough to hold the Ping-Pong ball.

Different concepts can be practiced with this game format. Perhaps the children need to practice counting by multiples such as 3s, 4s, 5s, or 6s instead of 10s. Another idea is to write addition or subtraction facts inside the holes. The player must solve the problem before rolling the marble or Ping-Pong ball into the hole. One point can be given for each correct answer and a second point for correctly rolling the ball or marble into the hole. The player with the most points can be declared the winner.

Marble Maze Pattern

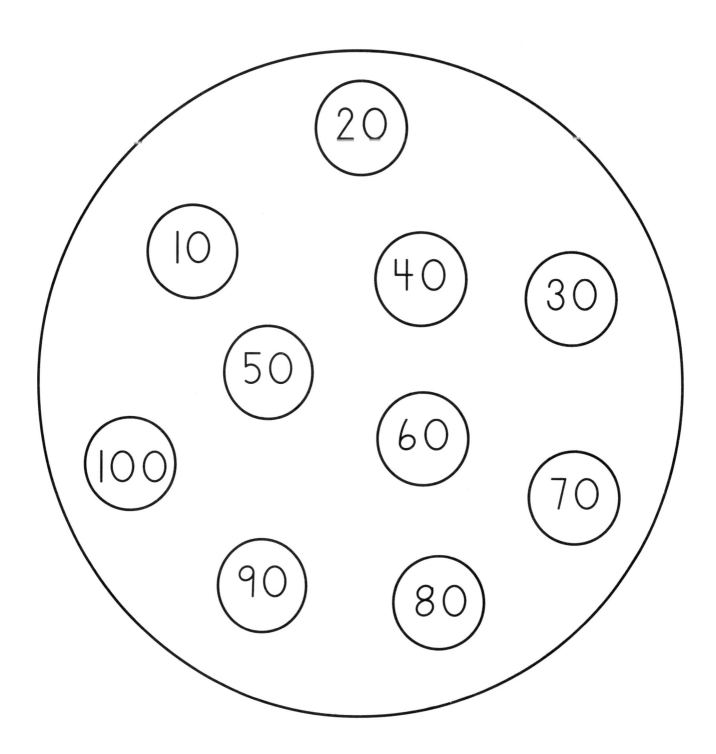

Marble Maze Pattern

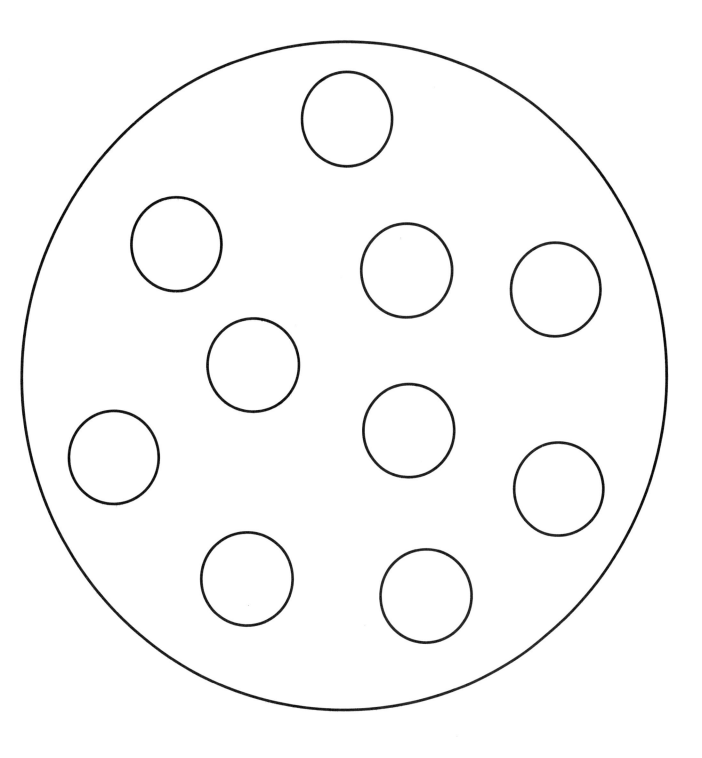

SPORTS NUMBERS

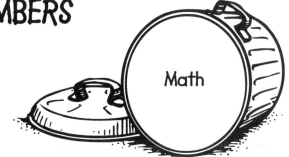

Skill:
Greater than/less than

Materials Needed:
- 1¼" (31 mm) round labels (optional)
- construction paper
- milk jug caps (either screw-on or snap-on lids)
- pattern page 191
- pictures (from magazines, newspapers, and catalogs) that show shirts with team numbers
- permanent marker
- glue
- scissors

Directions for Assembly:
1. Photocopy the pattern on construction paper. You will need one sheet of construction paper for every two pictures you have collected.
2. Select two pictures for each activity card and glue them in place. Arrange the pictures so that the activity cards vary. Some cards begin with larger numbers while others begin with smaller numbers.
3. Using a permanent marker, draw the > sign on the top of the milk cap, one per activity card. If the lid is not plain, cover it with a round label and then draw the > sign on the label.

How to Play:
1. Let three or four children play the game, giving each player a milk cap with the > or < sign on it and a game card.
2. Each child must determine which number is greater and then place the sign correctly.
3. Encourage the children to take turns reading their game cards while others listen.
4. When everyone is finished with the task, give each child a different game card.
5. Play continues until all of the game cards have been completed.

Other Ideas!
Duplicate pattern pages 192–193 and mount them on a file folder. Collect 30 milk jug caps and print numbers on them that are appropriate for the students to compare. To play the game, have the children work with partners. Place the numbered bottle caps *face down* in the center of the playing area. Each player takes a turn drawing a milk jug cap and placing it on the game board if it completes a comparison. Return the milk jug cap to the draw pile if not appropriate. Continue playing until a player completes one of the paths on the game board with numbers.

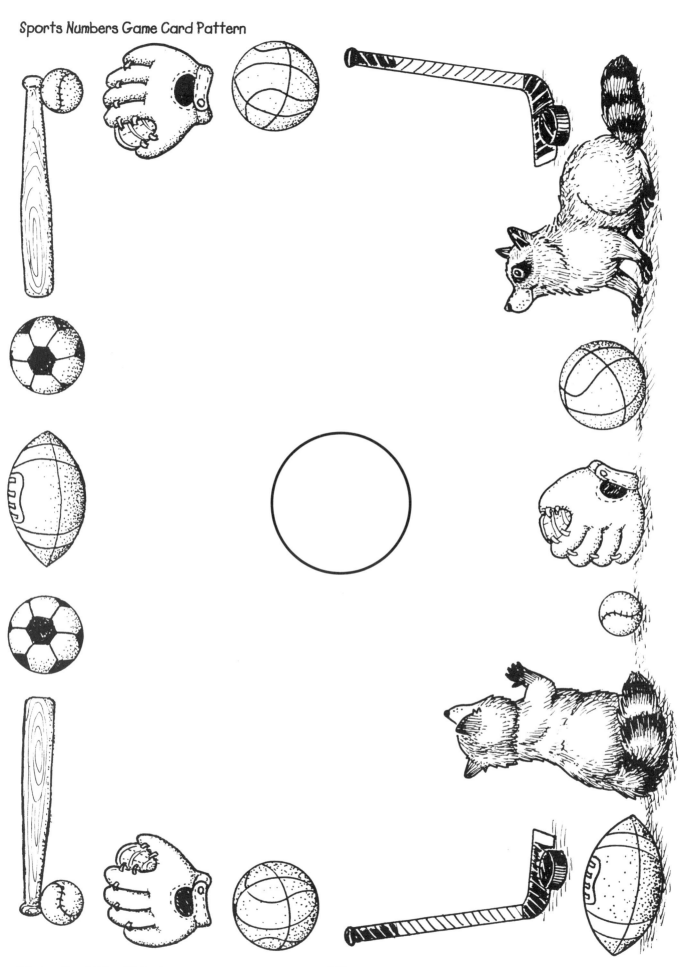

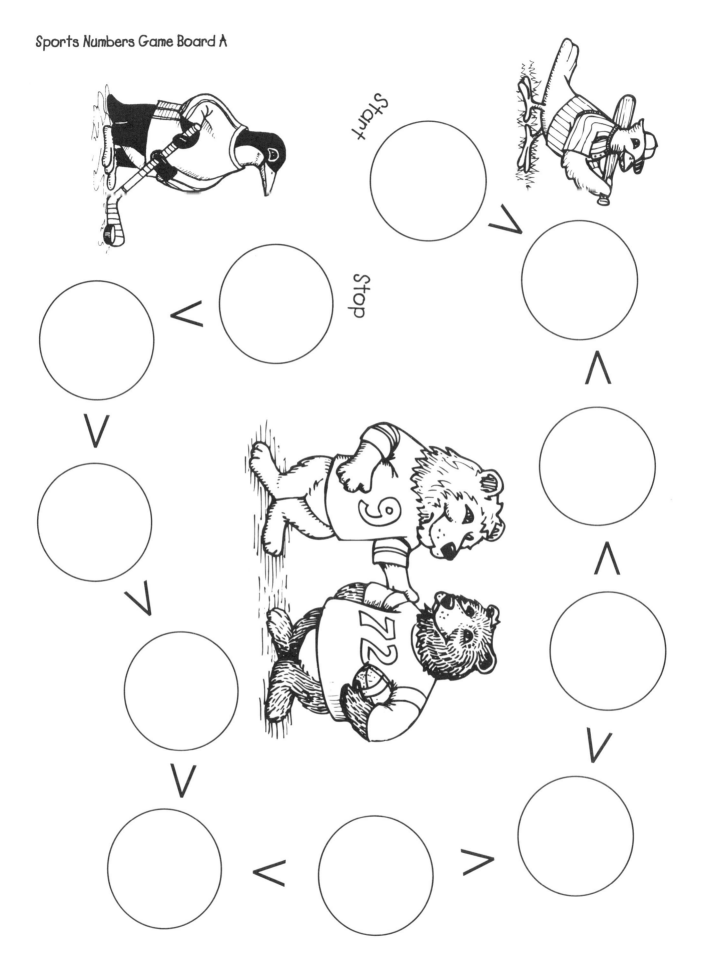

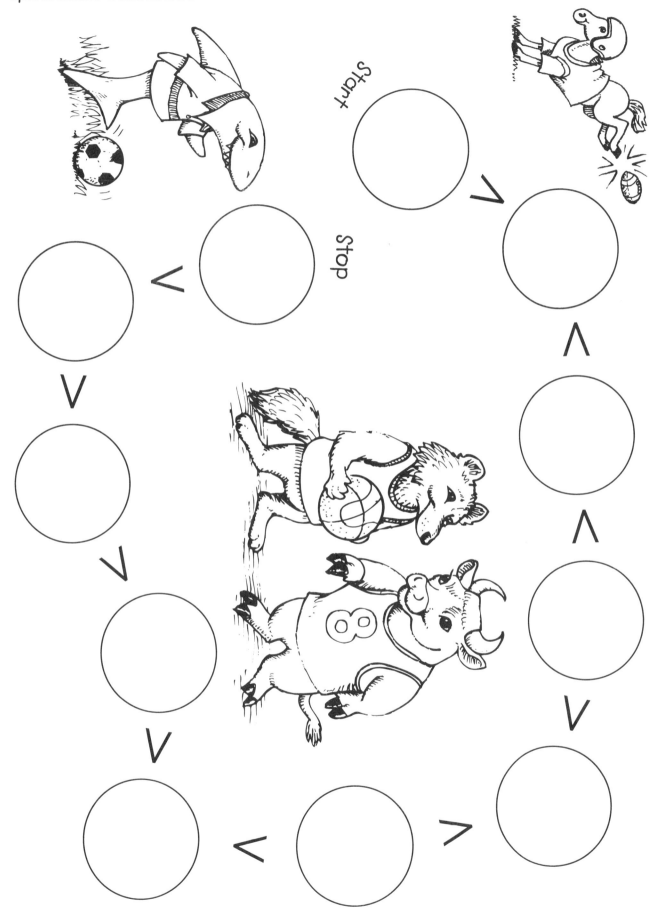

FEED THE MONSTER

Math

Skill:
Addition facts (sums to 10)

Materials Needed:
- clear adhesive plastic or laminating material
- glue
- one powdered detergent box (approximately 3 lb. or 1.36 kg)
- pattern pages 195–199
- permanent markers
- scissors

Directions for Assembly:
1. Cover the detergent box with contact paper.
2. Using the pattern on page 195, make a monster face. Color it with markers and then cover it with clear adhesive plastic.
3. Mount the monster to the front of the box. Glue the top of the head to the lid of the box and the bottom of the head to the front of the box directly under the opening. This will create a mouth for the monster.
4. Copy the cookie patterns on pages 196–198. Place a small sticker or dot on the backs of those sums that are correct. This will make the game self-checking.
5. Laminate the cookies for durability and cut apart.

How to Play:
1. Let a small group of children pretend to feed the monster. To begin play, scatter the cookies randomly near the monster.
2. The first child selects a cookie and determines if the sum is correct or not. If the sum is correct, the player feeds the monster. If the sum is incorrect, have the child set the cookie aside. If the child makes an incorrect decision, return the cookie to the center of the playing area.
3. Play continues until all of the cookies have been sorted.

Other Ideas!
This game can be used with a large group of children if there are enough cookies so each child may take a turn. This activity also works well in a center for children who prefer to work independently. If you wish to create your own monster cookies, use pattern page 200 for additional game cards.

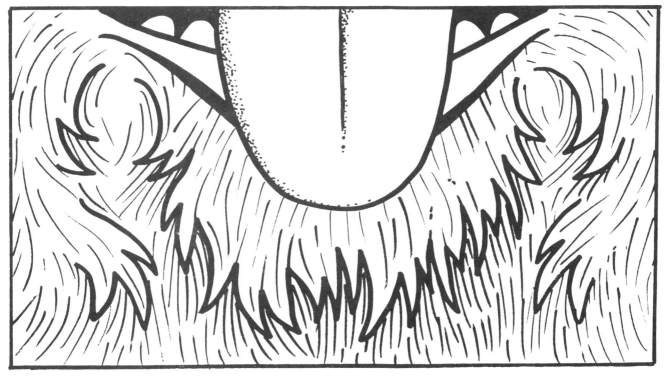

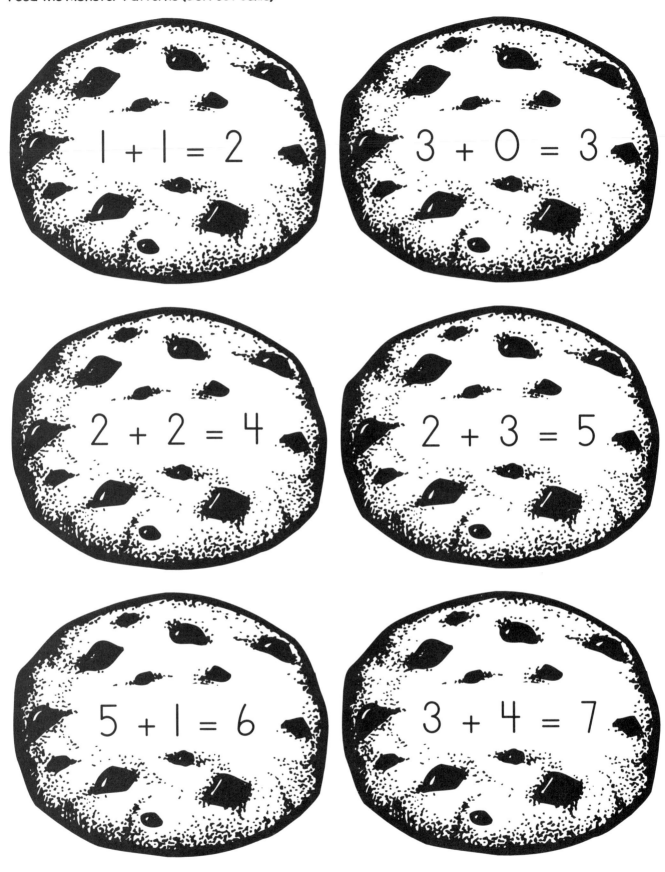

$1 + 1 = 2$

$3 + 0 = 3$

$2 + 2 = 4$

$2 + 3 = 5$

$5 + 1 = 6$

$3 + 4 = 7$

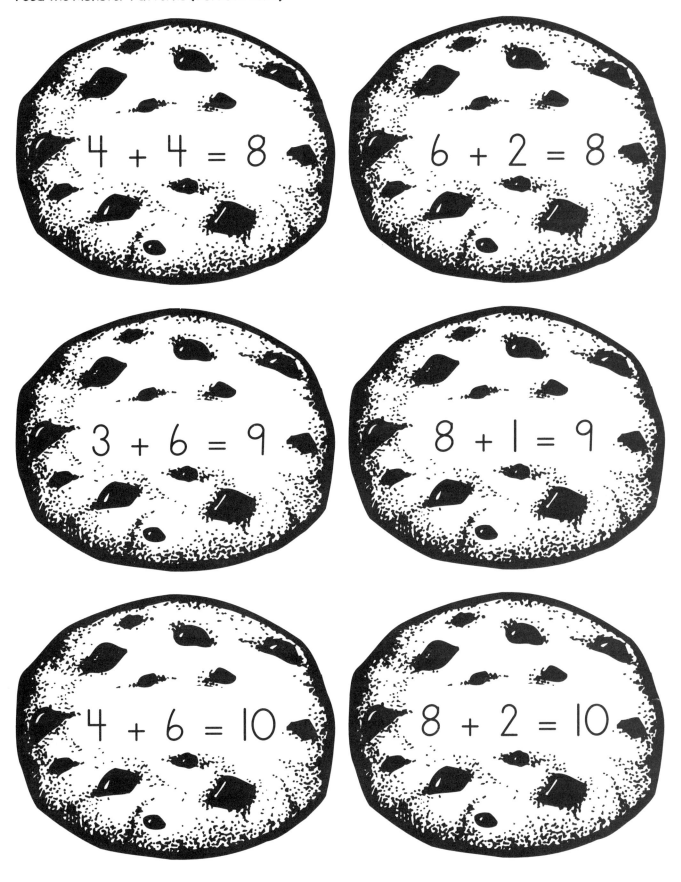

$4 + 4 = 8$

$6 + 2 = 8$

$3 + 6 = 9$

$8 + 1 = 9$

$4 + 6 = 10$

$8 + 2 = 10$

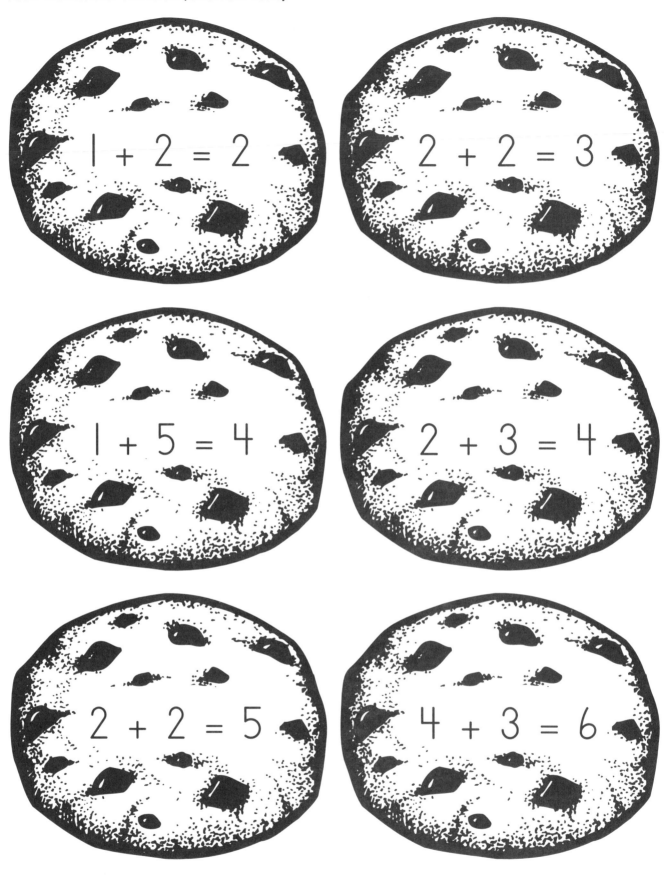

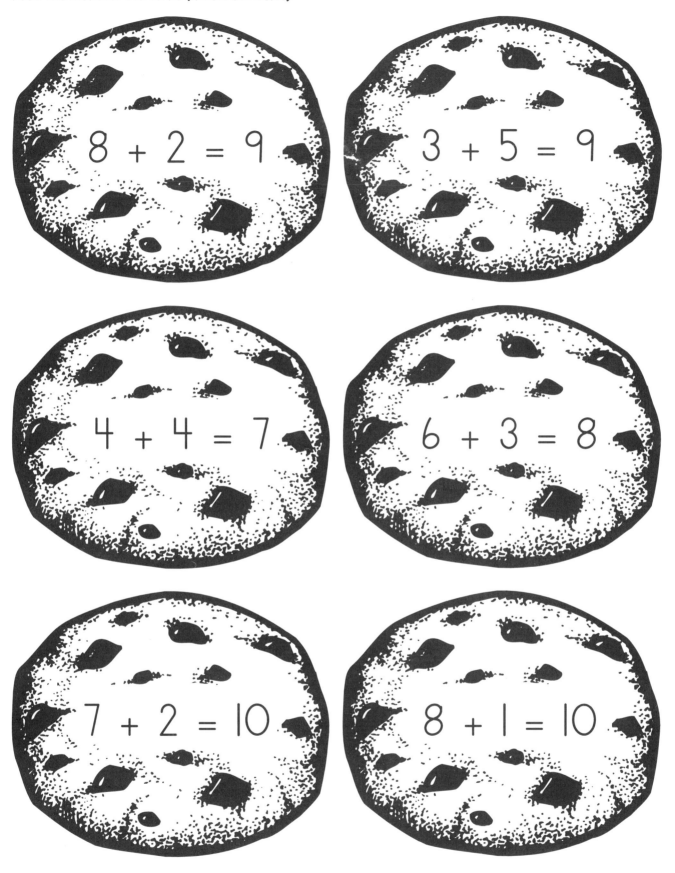

8 + 2 = 9

3 + 5 = 9

4 + 4 = 7

6 + 3 = 8

7 + 2 = 10

8 + 1 = 10

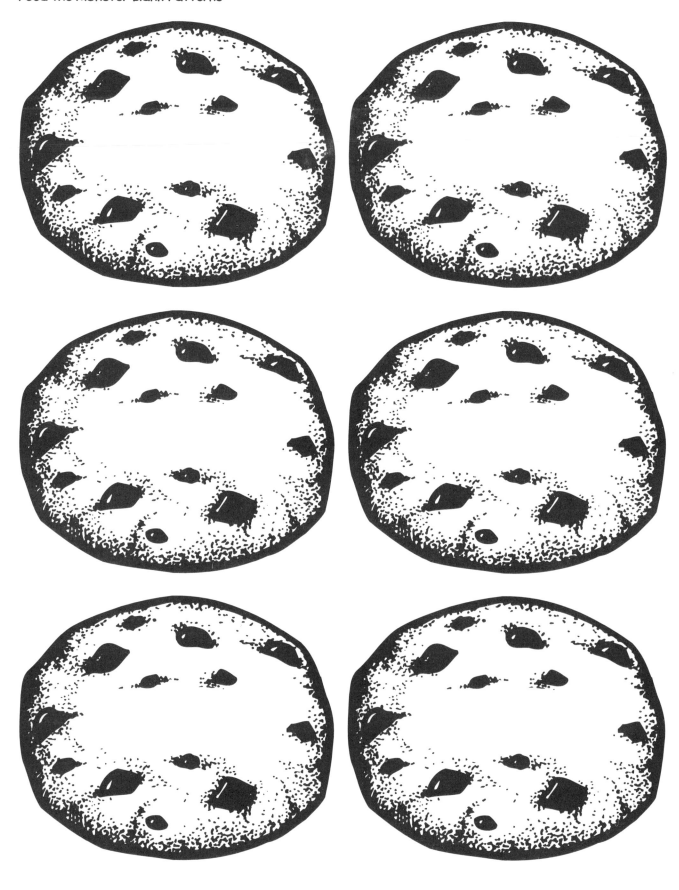

BUTTONS AND DOTS

Skill:
Simple addition

Math

Materials Needed:
- 20 various colored dot stickers, ¾" (19 mm) in size (or an assortment of stickers)
- collection of 20 or 40 buttons (any shape, color, or size)
- four school lunch milk cartons
- laminating material and/or clear adhesive plastic
- pattern pages 202–203
- permanent black marker and scissors

Directions for Assembly:
1. Photocopy pattern page 202 on construction paper, one per player.
2. Place a colored dot sticker or any other sticker in each box on the ten-frame grid. Laminate the grid page for durability.
3. For children who are able to work with larger numbers, provide grid cards by making photocopies of pattern page 203 on construction paper.
4. To make the dice, cut off the top of each milk carton. Push one carton inside the other carton to create a cube. Cover each cube with clear or plain colored adhesive plastic.
5. Using the permanent black marker write the numbers 0–5 on each cube to finish preparing the dice.

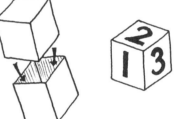

How to Play:
1. Let two children play the game. Direct the children to sit facing each other. Place a ten-frame gird or large grid card (20 boxes) in front of each child and the container with buttons in the middle.
2. The first child rolls the dice, adds the two numbers shown on the dice and covers the corresponding number of boxes with buttons on the strip or grid. The second child repeats the same procedure.
3. Play continues until one child has covered an entire grid with buttons. Exact numbers must be rolled to finish filling the grid.

Other Ideas!
Perhaps your students are ready for more challenging activities. Photocopy pattern page 162 for each player. Place a sticker in each empty box. Taking turns, let each player add the numbers shown on the dice when rolled and then cover the sticker above the corresponding numeral on the game card. Play until the entire grid is covered.

Button and Dots Pattern

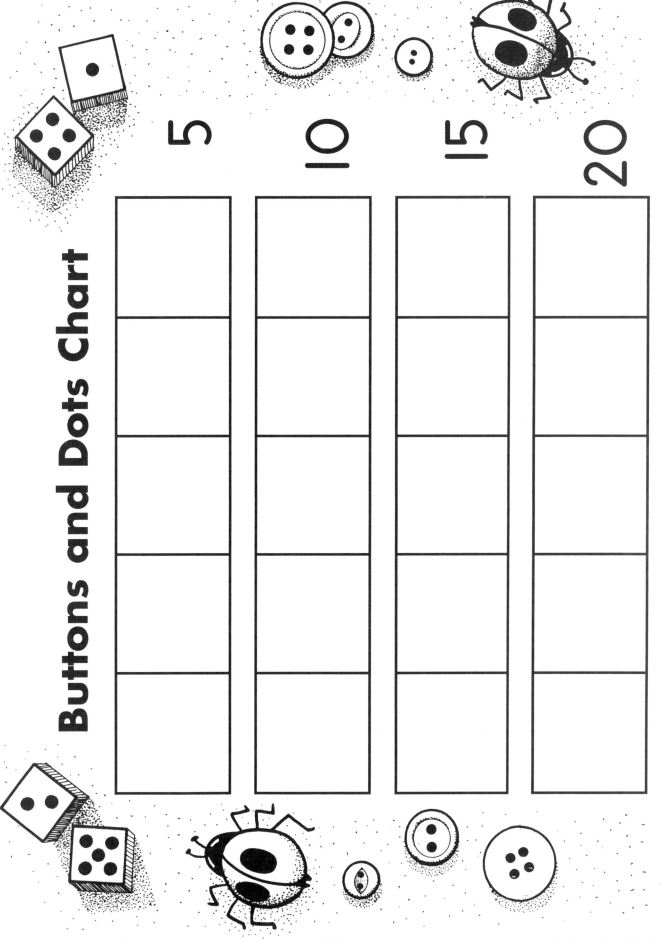

Buttons and Dots Chart

5	10	15	20

CREEPY CRAWLERS INSIDE THE BOX

Math

Skill:
Beginning addition

Materials Needed:
- 12 sheets of white construction paper
- 36 small plastic spiders and insects
  or any small items (buttons, macaroni, pennies)
- laminating material
- pattern pages 205–217
- pencils
- shirt box

Directions for Assembly:
1. Copy each task card pattern onto a sheet of white construction paper and laminate.
2. Make several copies of the student recording sheet.
3. Place the task cards, the plastic figures or whatever items you selected to use as "Creepy Crawlers," and copies of the student recording sheet in the box. Decorate the cover of the box as desired.

How to Play:
1. Invite two children to play the game.
2. Give each child 18 plastic creatures, a recording sheet, and a pencil.
3. Each child selects a task card and then places a "Creepy Crawler" on each "X."
4. Let the child find the sum of plastic creatures on the task card by adding the number inside the box with those outside the box.
5. Have the children record the number sentences on their recording sheets that match the numbers on their task cards.
6. When finished, encourage each child to select another task card and continue in the same manner.
7. Play continues until each child has completed a predetermined number of task cards.

Other Ideas!
If appropriate, provide task cards for addition facts (sums to 20), using the blank task card pattern (see pages 218-219). Have the children complete the activity in the same manner.

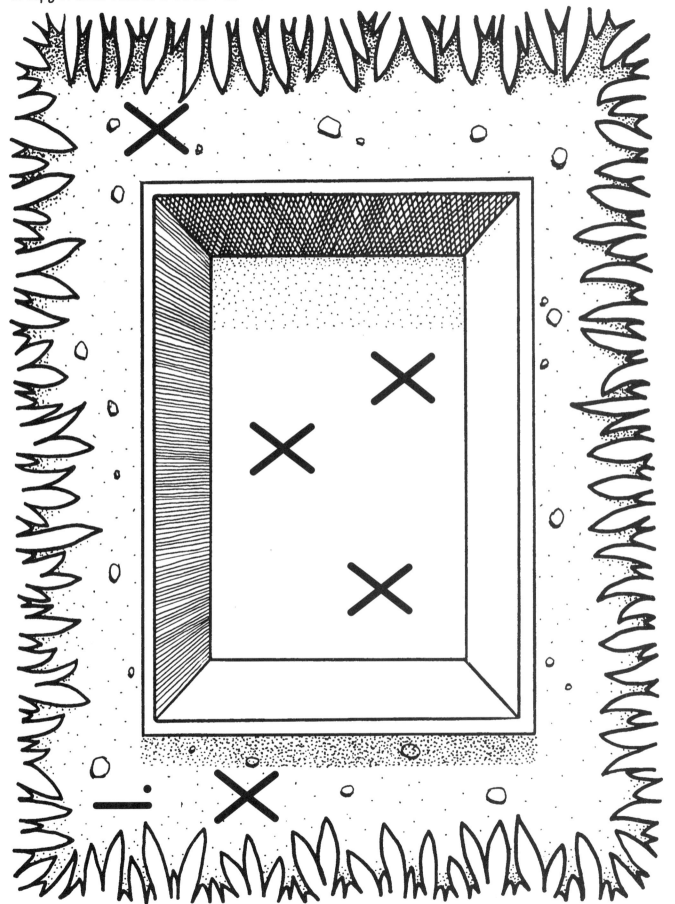

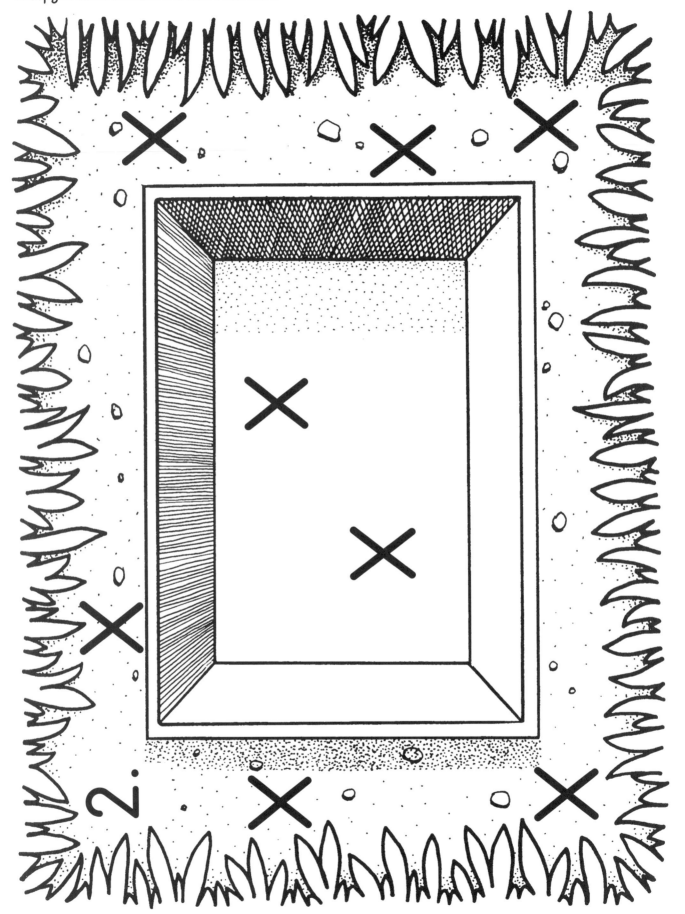

2.

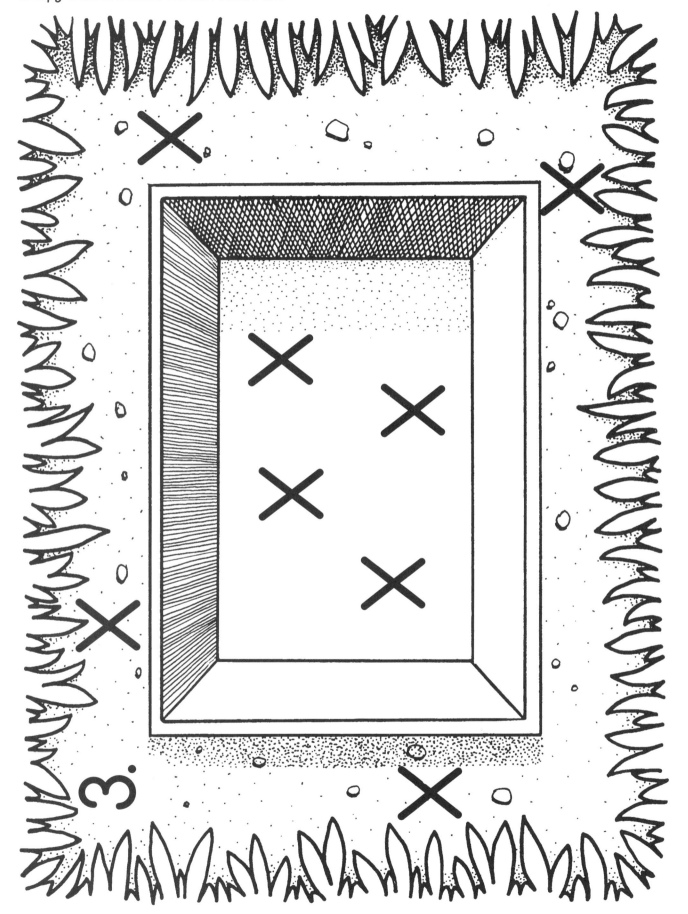

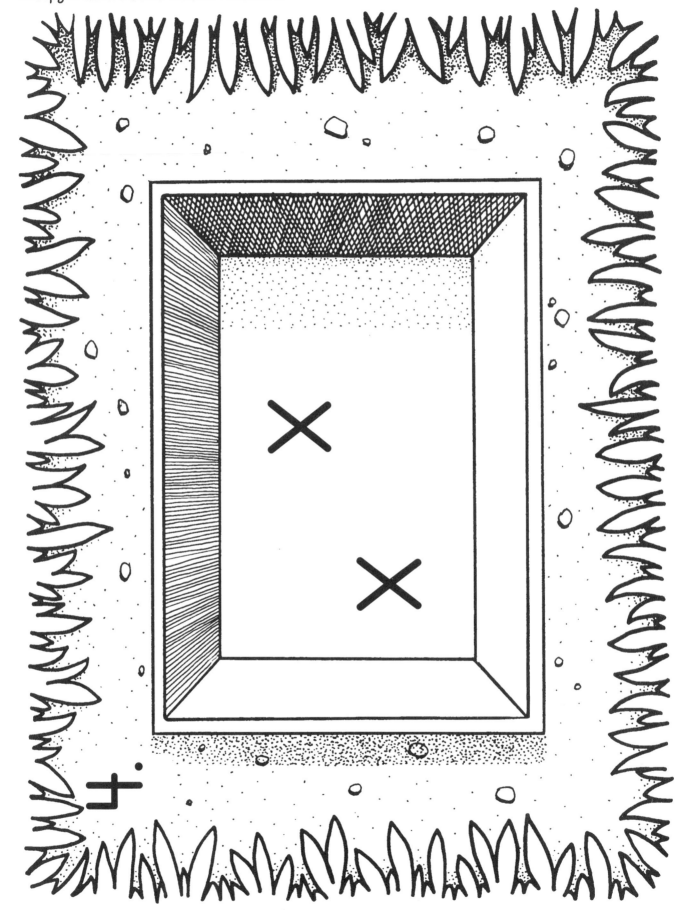

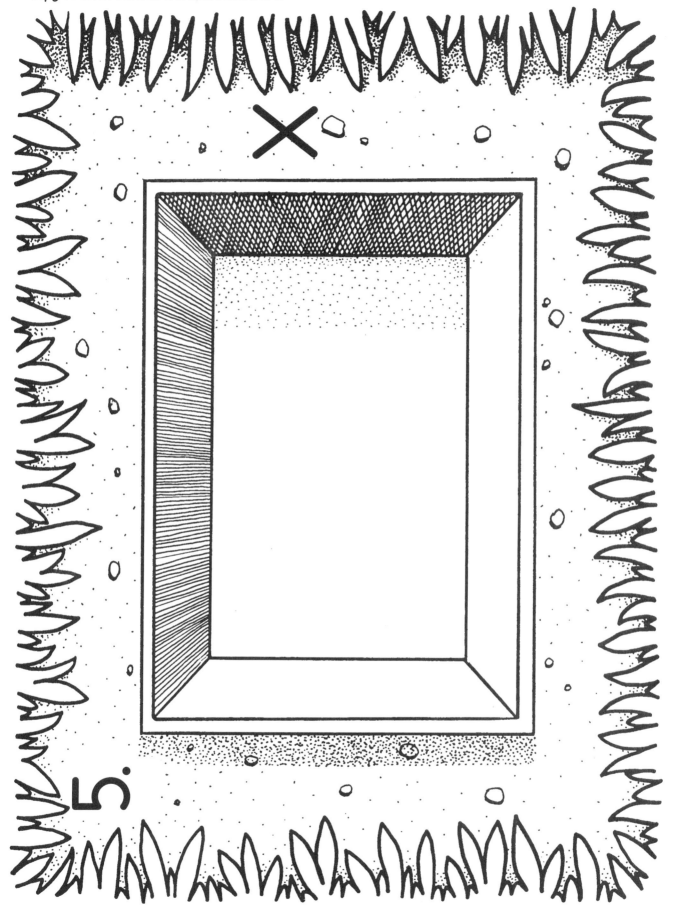

5.

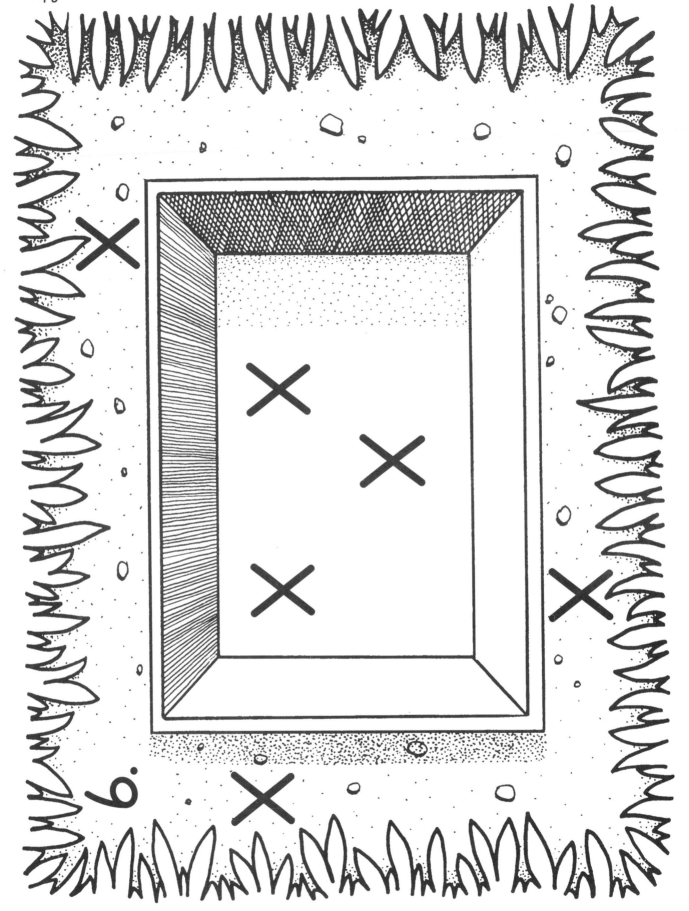

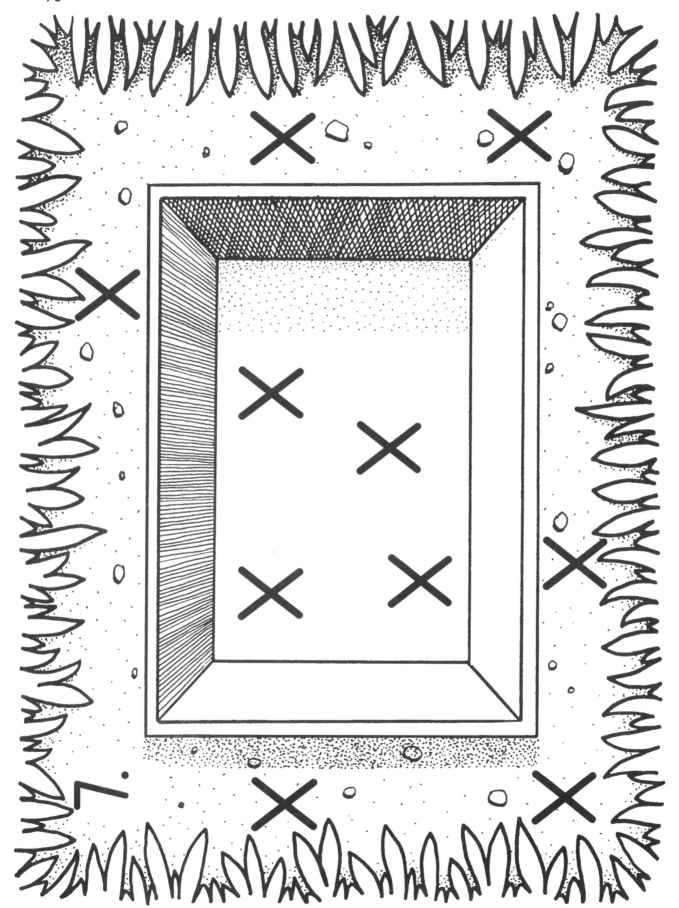

Creepy Crawlers inside the Box Task Card

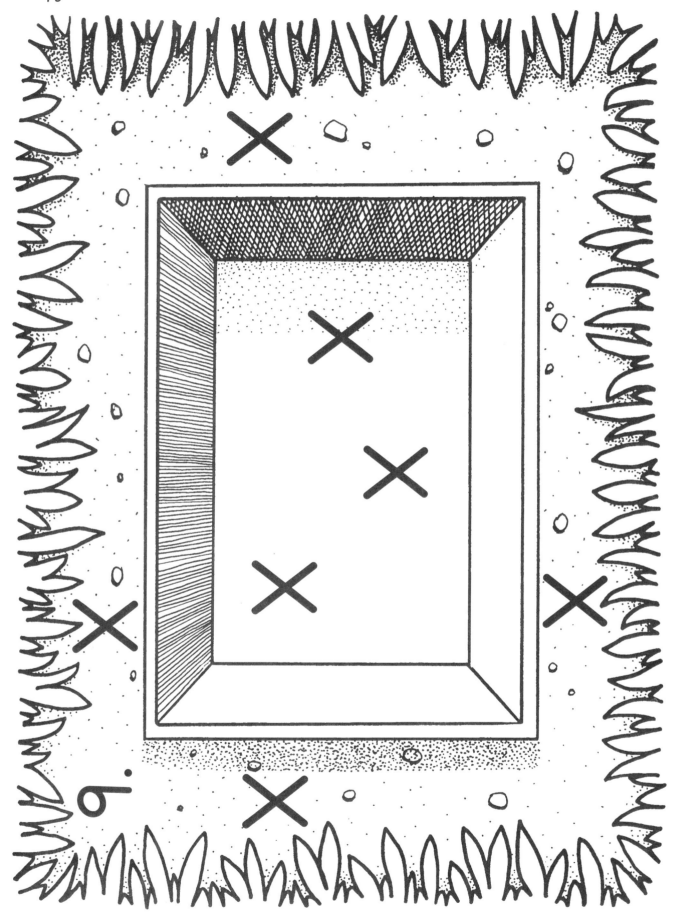

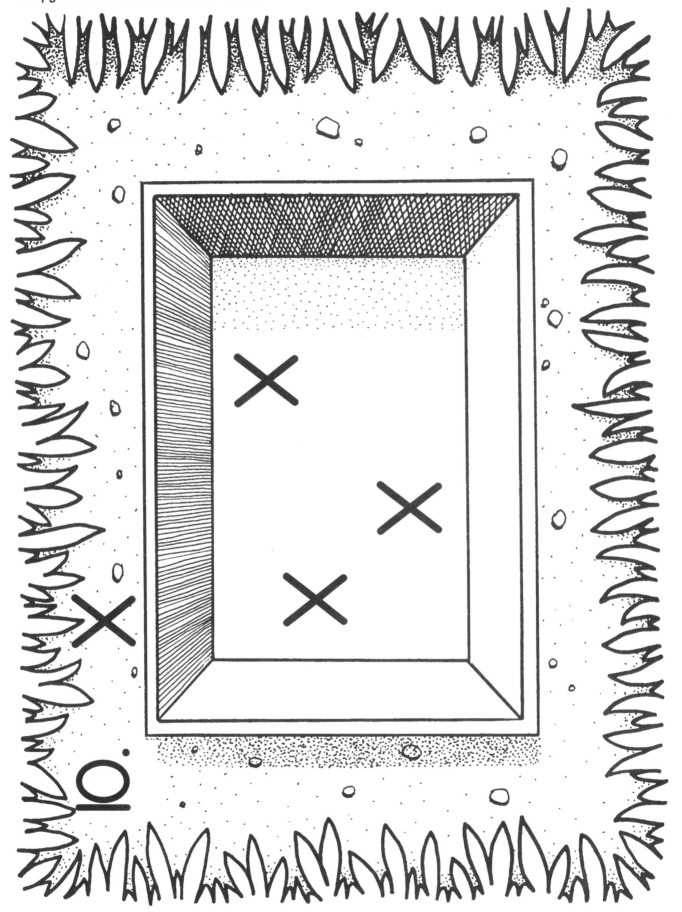

Creepy Crawlers inside the Box Task Card

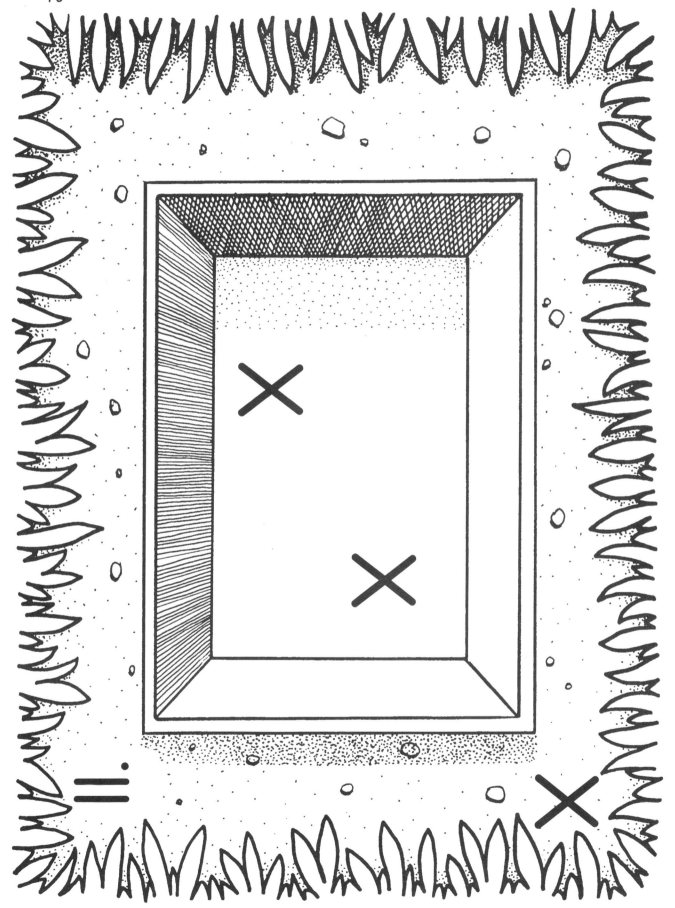

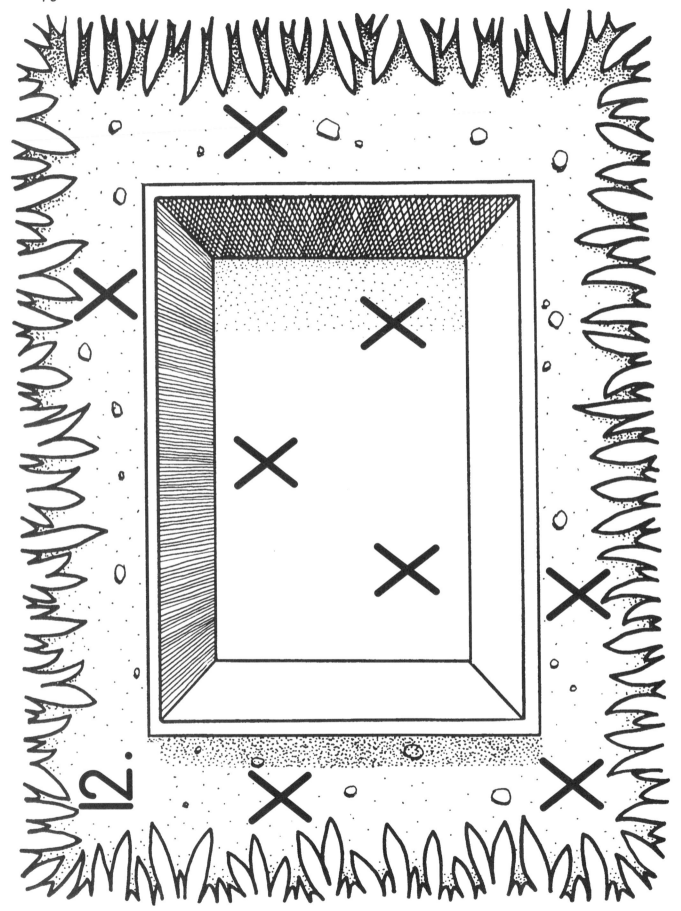

Creepy Crawlers inside the Box Recording Sheet

1.

□ + _____ = _____

2.

_____ + □ = _____

3.

□ + _____ = _____

4.

_____ + □ = _____

5.

□ + _____ = _____

6.

_____ + □ = _____

7.

□ + _____ = _____

8.

_____ + □ = _____

9.

□ + _____ = _____

10.

_____ + □ = _____

11.

□ + _____ = _____

12.

_____ + □ = _____

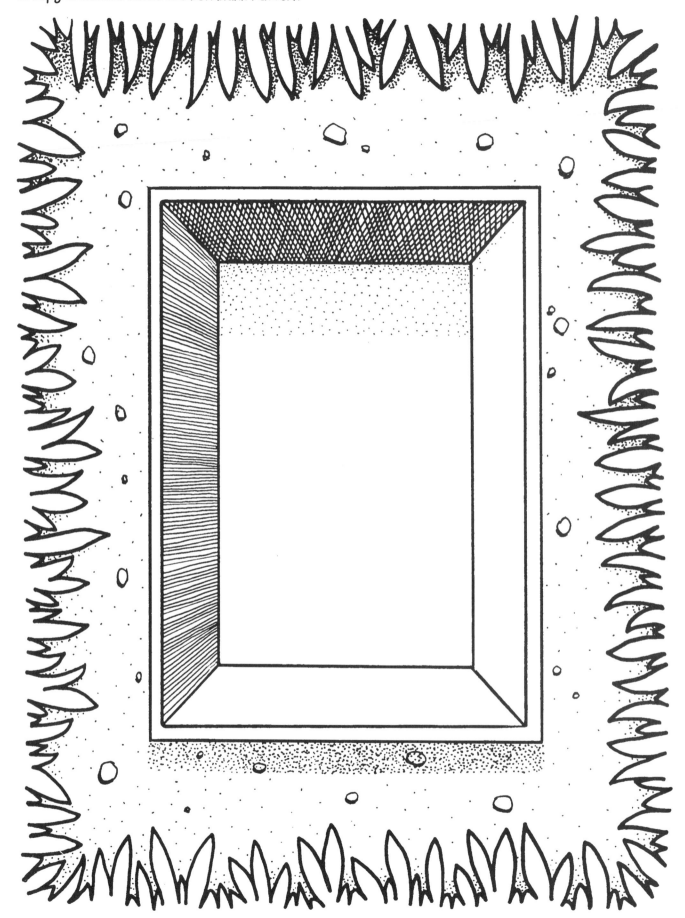

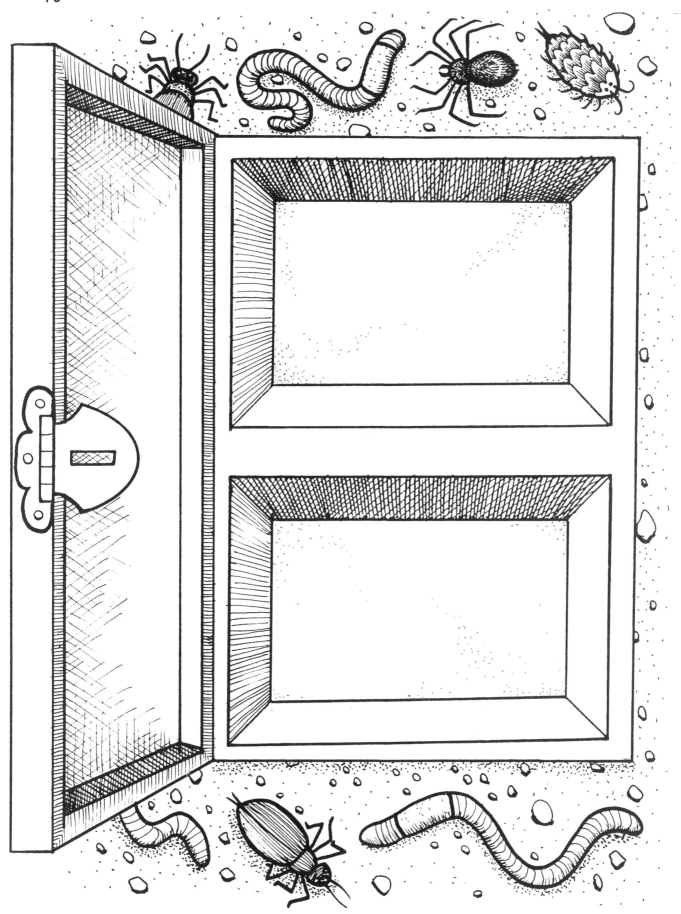

TIC-TAC-TOE

Math

Skill:
Addition facts

Materials Needed:
- buttons, washers, or any small round objects
- construction paper
- floor tile spacers (available at hardware or lumber stores)
- large resealable plastic bags, one for each game board
- one empty sticker sheet for each pair of students playing the game, each sheet has three empty spaces across and three spaces down
- pattern pages 221–225

Directions for Assembly:
1. Cut construction paper to match the size of the sticker sheet, approximately 4½" x 5½" (115 x 140 mm). Prepare one piece of construction paper for each sticker sheet.
2. Separate the sticker sheet from the backing and mount the frame on the construction paper. This will provide the backing for the tic-tac-toe board. The empty sticker spaces provide the grid for the tic-tac-toe game pieces.
3. Photocopy the game cards (pages 221–225) on construction paper, one set per game board. Cut apart the cards. Select the addition facts that are appropriate for the children and set the remaining cards aside for future use. If appropriate, make additional game cards (see page 225).
4. Place a game board, a set of game cards, five floor tile spacers, and five buttons or washers into each resealable bag.

How to Play:
1. Give each pair of children game pieces and a game board which is placed between them.
2. One child use the floor tiles (Xs) and the other child uses the buttons (Os) for game markers.
3. The game cards are placed *face down* in a pile near the game board.
4. The first player draws a game card. If the child correctly answers the addition problem, a game marker is placed on a chosen space, then the other player takes a turn.
5. Play continues until one player has placed three game markers in a vertical, horizontal, or diagonal row. That player is the winner. If all of the spaces are filled and no one has three markers in a row, the board is cleared.

Other Ideas!
The game can be changed to reinforce other skills—number words, subtraction problems, and so on.

0 + 1	8 + 1
1 + 1	2 + 0
2 + 1	1 + 2
3 + 1	2 + 2
4 + 1	3 + 2
5 + 1	4 + 2
6 + 1	5 + 2
7 + 1	6 + 2

7 + 2	4 + 0
0 + 3	1 + 4
1 + 3	2 + 4
2 + 3	3 + 4
3 + 3	4 + 4
4 + 3	5 + 4
5 + 3	0 + 5
6 + 3	1 + 5

7 + 3	9 + 4
8 + 3	5 + 5
9 + 3	6 + 5
8 + 2	7 + 5
9 + 2	8 + 5
6 + 4	9 + 5
7 + 4	4 + 6
8 + 4	5 + 6

2 + 5	1 + 7
3 + 5	2 + 7
4 + 5	3 + 7
6 + 0	8 + 0
1 + 6	1 + 8
2 + 6	9 + 0
3 + 6	6 + 6
0 + 7	0 + 0

7 + 6	
8 + 6	
9 + 6	
7 + 8	
9 + 7	
8 + 8	
9 + 8	
9 + 9	

WHEELBARROW RACES

Skill:
Subtraction facts

Math

Materials Needed:
- clear adhesive plastic or laminating materials
- four paper fasteners
- four plastic snap-off lids from milk or water jugs
- glue
- hole punch
- markers
- one colored file folder
- pattern pages 228–233
- scissors
- craft knife
- two plastic scoops from powdered laundry detergent boxes

Directions for Assembly:
1. To make the wheelbarrows, punch a hole on two opposite sides of the plastic laundry scoop.
2. Using the craft knife, make a small slit in the middle of each milk cap. Push the paper fastener through the slit, then through the hole in the plastic scoop to create the wheels.

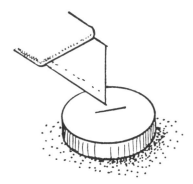

3. Photocopy the game board patterns. Color the circles for the wheelbarrow path, using one color for one path and a second color for the other path. Decorate as desired with markers, cut around the pieces that will pop up, and then mount the sheets onto the file folder.
4. Cover the folder with clear adhesive plastic. Recut around the pop-up pieces.
5. To prepare the game cards, photocopy the pattern pages 230–233 on construction paper. If appropriate, make additional game cards (see page 233).
6. Laminate the cards and then cut them apart.

How to Play:

1. Invite two children to play the game.
2. Each child selects a wheelbarrow and a path to use. The wheelbarrow is placed on the first circle on the path.
3. Place the game cards *face down* in the center box. Be sure to select the subtraction facts which are appropriate for the children and set the remaining cards aside for future use.
4. Each player draws a game card from the pile and solves the equation. The player with the largest difference will start the game.
5. The first player draws a card and solves the equation. If the answer is correct, the player moves the wheelbarrow to the next circle on the path. If the answer is incorrect, the card is placed on the bottom of the pile and the child loses a turn.
6. Play continues until a wheelbarrow arrives at the last circle on the path.

Other Ideas!

You can create your own games cards that reinforce skills such as color or number words, basic sight words, addition facts, place value, spelling words, question/answer cards for science, and so on. The possiblities are endless for extra practice.

Stop

Place game cards here.

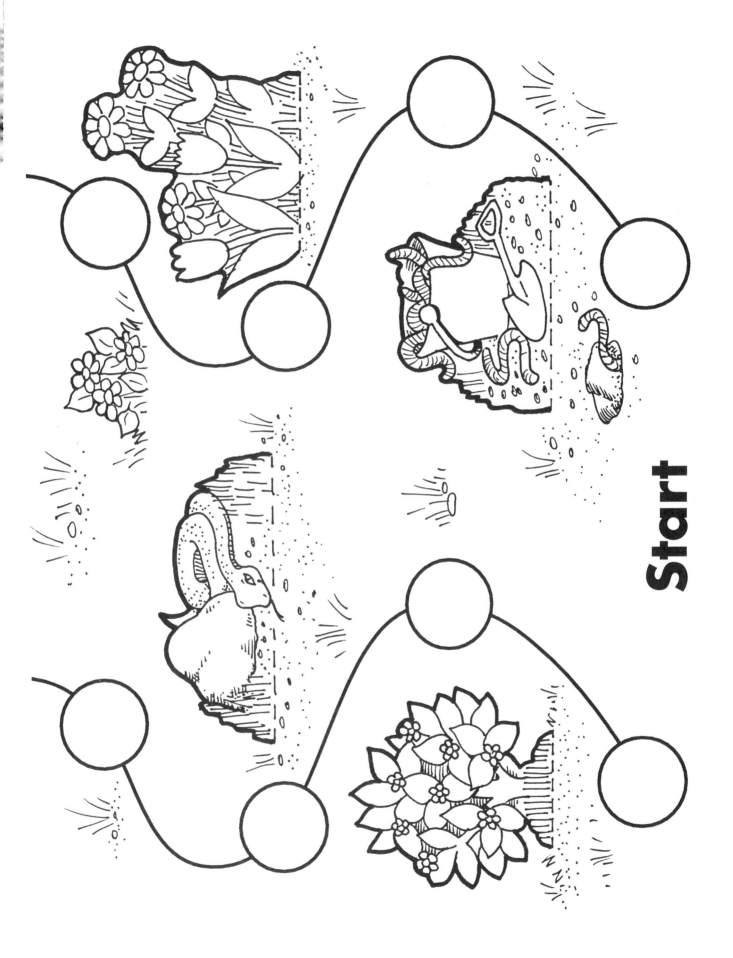

Start

$9 - 0 =$	$9 - 1 =$
$9 - 2 =$	$9 - 3 =$
$9 - 4 =$	$9 - 5 =$
$9 - 6 =$	$9 - 7 =$
$9 - 8 =$	$9 - 9 =$
$8 - 0 =$	$8 - 1 =$
$8 - 2 =$	$8 - 3 =$
$8 - 4 =$	$8 - 5 =$

8 – 6 =	8 – 7 =
8 – 8 =	7 – 0 =
7 – 1 =	7 – 2 =
7 – 3 =	7 – 4 =
7 – 5 =	7 – 6 =
7 – 7 =	6 – 0 =
6 – 1 =	6 – 2 =
6 – 3 =	6 – 4 =

15 – 9 =	12 – 9 =
14 – 9 =	12 – 8 =
14 – 8 =	12 – 7 =
14 – 7 =	12 – 6 =
14 – 6 =	11 – 9 =
13 – 9 =	11 – 8 =
13 – 8 =	11 – 7 =
13 – 7 =	11 – 6 =

10 − 9 =	10 − 6 =
10 − 8 =	10 − 5 =
10 − 7 =	15 − 8 =
15 − 7 =	15 − 6 =

LET'S BOWL!

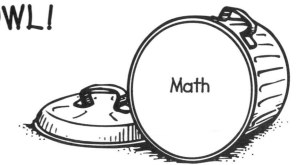

Skill:
Subtraction facts

Materials Needed:
- ten half-gallon (1.89 L) plastic milk containers or two-liter soda bottles
- 60 paper fasteners
- hole punch
- laminating material
- pattern page 236
- scissors
- six sheets of dark construction paper, 5½" x 24" (14 x 61 cm) in size
- 12 sheets of white construction paper
- small beanbag

Directions for Assembly:
1. Duplicate 12 copies of the bowling pin pattern page on white construction paper.
2. Laminate the bowling pins and the six sheets of dark construction paper.
3. Cut out the bowling pins.
4. Place ten bowling pins in a row, spacing them evenly, on each sheet of dark construction paper.
5. Using the hole punch, punch a hole through the bowling pin and the dark construction paper. Secure the bowling pin in place with a paper fastener. Repeat the procedure with the remaining pins.

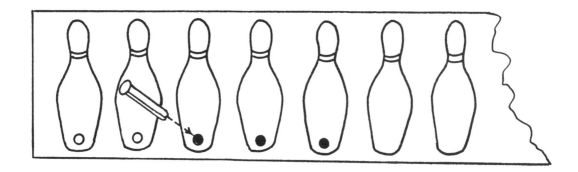

How to Play:
1. Select a place to play and set up the milk bottles or soda bottles within a triangular shape on the floor. Place a mark on the floor, a few feet back, with a small piece of tape or something similar. This will mark the spot where the child stands when throwing the beanbag.

2. Allow three to six children to play the game.
3. Each child takes a place on either side of the playing area (a safe distance from any moving bottles) along with a game board.
4. The first player stands on the taped line and throws the beanbag, trying to knock down as many "pins" as possible.
5. Have the player count the pins which are no longer standing. Each child "knocks" over the same number of pins on her/his game board.
6. The remaining pins that are still standing are counted.
7. Let each child have an opportunity to say the number sentence that was created. Example: "We had ten pins and Karla knocked down three. That leaves seven pins."
8. Each child returns the pins on the game board to an upright position.
9. The next player takes a turn at tossing the beanbag.
10. Play continues until everyone has had several turns or until a predetermined amount of time ends.

Other Ideas!
Have the children write the number sentences on individual chalkboards while playing the game.

Let's Bowl! Pattern

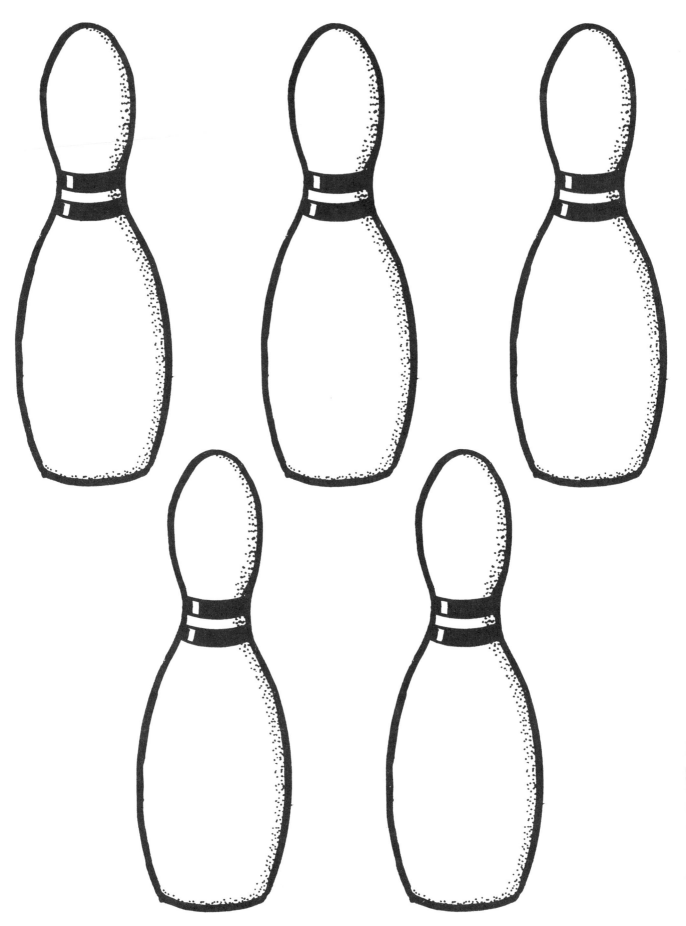

236   IF18974 *Quick Games from Trash*

RINGS ON YOUR FINGERS

Math

Skill:
Simple subtraction

Materials Needed:
- 16 children's novelty rings
  (have flat surfaces for writing on them)
- tan construction paper
- clear adhesive plastic
- glue
- one shirt or dress box
- pattern page 238
- permanent marker
- scissors
- craft knife

Directions for Assembly:
1. Using the craft knife, cut each corner of the box lid and bottom so that the panels will lay flat.
2. Copy 16 handprints on tan construction paper and cut them out.
3. Mount eight handprints on the box lid and eight on the box bottom.
4. Cover both panels with clear adhesive plastic. Using small strips of the adhesive plastic, tape the corners of the boxes to reinforce the box lid and box bottom.
5. Using the craft knife, cut a small rectangle on the ring finger of each handprint. It should be large enough to hold the novelty ring in place as it rests on the box surface.
6. Using the permanent marker, write subtraction equations that are appropriate for the children on the handprints.
7. Finish preparing the materials by writing the answers to the equations on the rings. Place the rings inside the box along with an answer key.

How to Play:
Solve the equations and place the appropriate rings on the corresponding handprints.

Other Ideas!
If you would like to reuse the rings with different equations, erase the answers with fingernail polish remover. Some children may be ready to work with mixed equations (addition and subtraction facts).

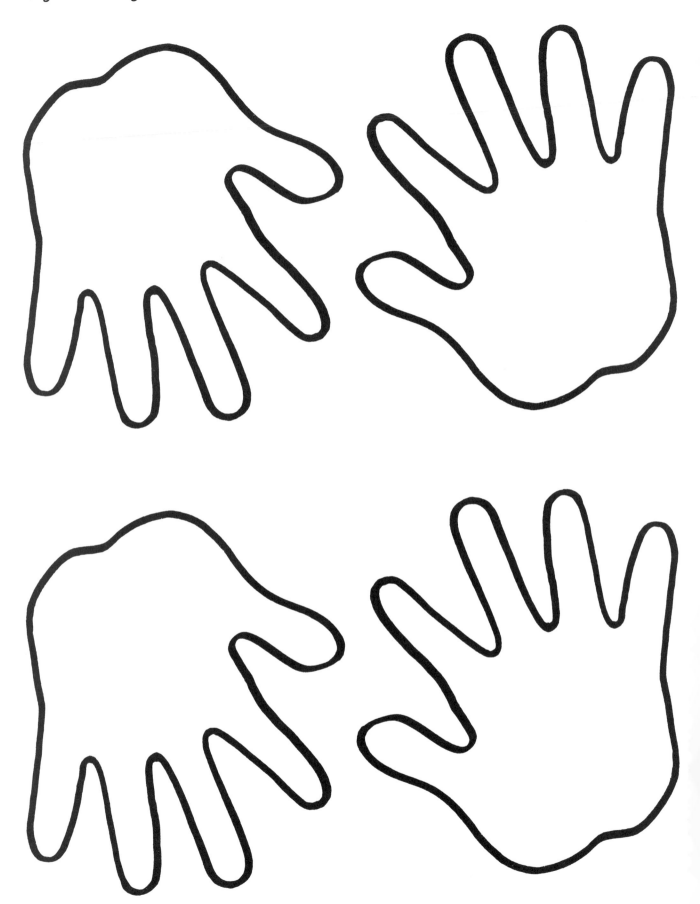

SHAKE, SHAKE!

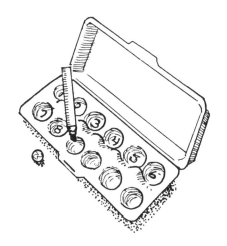

Math

Skill:
Graphing

Materials Needed:
- crayons
- egg carton
- lima bean, marble, or any other small object
- pattern page 240
- permanent marker

Directions for Assembly:
1. Using the permanent marker, write a number in each egg cup.
2. Place a dried bean, marble, or small object inside the carton and close.

How to Play:
1. Ask a small group of children to play the game. Give each child a crayon and a recording sheet.
2. The first child begins by shaking the egg carton several times, opens the lid, and then names the number where the bean rests.
3. The first player records that number on his recording sheet by coloring one box above the corresponding numeral.
4. The egg carton is passed to the next player who repeats the process.
5. Play continues until each child has recorded ten turns.
6. Let the children compare their graphs. Find out which number was colored the most times and which one was colored the fewest times.

Other Ideas!
This "Shake, Shake" game can also be used for practicing addition. To prepare the materials, number the egg cups 0–5 in each row. Place two small objects inside the egg carton and close it. This time when the player shakes and opens the carton, have her or him add the two numbers together and announce the sum. Use the recording sheet to track which sums were identified. Some children may wish to work with larger sums. Prepare the egg carton by printing 0–5 and 4–9 in the egg cups. Make a recording sheet that reflects the possible sums.

Shake, Shake! Pattern

							10
							9
							8
							7
							6
							5
							4
							3
							2
							1